Oxford
International
Primary

5

English
Student Book

Alison Barber
Izabella Hearn
Myra Murby

OXFORD

# OXFORD
## UNIVERSITY PRESS

Great Clarendon Street, Oxford, OX2 6DP, United Kingdom

Oxford University Press is a department of the University of Oxford. It furthers the University's objective of excellence in research, scholarship, and education by publishing worldwide. Oxford is a registered trade mark of Oxford University Press in the UK and in certain other countries.

British Library Cataloguing in Publication Data

Data available

ISBN 978-1-38-201987-3

7 9 10 8 6

Paper used in the production of this book is a natural, recyclable product made from wood grown in sustainable forests. The manufacturing process conforms to the environmental regulations of the country of origin.

Printed in China by Shanghai Offset Printing Products Ltd

## Acknowledgements

The publisher and authors would like to thank the following for permission to use photographs and other copyright material:

**Cover:** Artwork by Dan Gartman. **Photos: p3(t):** blickwinkel/Alamy Stock Photo; **p3(m):** Winchester College/In aid of Mary Seacole Memorial Statue Appeal/Mary Evans; **p3(b):** Marco Tomasini/Shutterstock; **p8(b):** Chris Driscoll/Shutterstock; **p8(bkgd):** Radius Images/Alamy Stock Photo; **p9(t):** YegoroV/Shutterstock; **p9(b):** irabel8/Shutterstock; **p11:** Dr. Ingmar Koehler/Shutterstock; **p12:** fon.tepsoda/Shutterstock; **p16-17(bkgd):** Seregam/Shutterstock; **p16-17:** Madlen/Shutterstock; **p16-17:** Olga Popova/Shutterstock; **p16-17:** Photodisc/Getty Images; **p17(b):** Ronstik/Shutterstock; **p25(t):** Zacarias Pereira Da Mata/123RF; **p25(b):** Tatiana Popova/Shutterstock; **p26(tl):** Konstantin Shaklein/Alamy Stock Photo; **p26(tr):** Evolution1088/Dreamstime; **p26(bl):** Look At Sciences/Science Photo Library; **p26(br):** Andi Duff/Alamy Stock Photo; **p27:** Hilary Morgan/Alamy Stock Photo; **p28(t):** Nick Greaves/Shutterstock; **p28(b):** Stubblefield Photography/Shutterstock; **p29:** Martin Harvey/Alamy Stock Photo; **p31:** View Stock/Alamy Stock Photo; **p32:** Melvyn Longhurst/Alamy Stock Photo; **p32-33(bkgd):** Getty Images; **p33:** Min C. Chiu/Shutterstock; **p35(tr):** Tomasz Markowski/Shutterstock; **p35(br):** Romolo Tavani/Shutterstock; **p35(bl):** PHOTOCREO Michal Bednarek/Shutterstock; **p36(bkgd):** R-studio/Shutterstock; **p36(bl):** Tristan tan/Shutterstock; **p36(br):** MaxPhotographer/Shutterstock; **p37(t):** Carolina Arroyo/Shutterstock; **p37(m):** GraphicPhotoArt -MomPhoto/Shutterstock; **p37(b):** Highviews/Shutterstock; **p38:** F1online digitale Bildagentur GmbH/Alamy Stock Photo; **p39:** Ian Shaw/Alamy Stock Photo; **p40(bkgd):** Photodisc/Getty Images; **p40(b):** Daniel Berehulak/Getty Images; **p41:** REUTERS/Alamy Stock Photo; **p42(t):** EyeWire/Getty Images; **p42(b):** Jan Tadeusz/OUP; **p44(t):** RR/Shutterstock; **p44(ml):** Phonlamai Photo/Shutterstock; **p44(mr):** Dmytro Zinkevych/Shutterstock; **p44(b):** Phonlamai Photo/Shutterstock; **p51:** Monkey Business Images/Shutterstock; **p52(l):** Chrisbrignell/Shutterstock; **p52(r):** RikoBest/Shutterstock; **p58(bkgd):** Altanaka/Shutterstock; **p58(bl):** Pamela June Crook/Bridgeman Images; **p59:** Hulton Archive/Getty Images; **p77:** Chin Kit Sen/Shutterstock; **p79(a):** sonia.eps/Shutterstock; **p79(b):** Cindy Lee/Shutterstock; **p79(c):** Mehmet Buma/Shutterstock; **p79(d):** Paul Stringer/Shutterstock; **p79(e):** 3D generator/Shutterstock; **p80:** Sergey Novikov/123RF; **p81:** Ol_dmi/Shutterstock; **p82(t):** Winchester College/In aid of Mary Seacole Memorial Statue Appeal/Mary Evans; **p82(b):** Marzolino/Shutterstock; **p83(l):** magicinfoto/Shutterstock; **p83(r):** Pump Park Vintage Photography/Alamy Stock Photo; **p83(bkgd):** Ratana21/Shutterstock; **p86(t):** Borja Suarez/Reuters; **p86(b):** REUTERS/Alamy Stock Photo; **p86(bkgd):** DOCTOR BLACK/Shutterstock; **p86(bkgd2):** airn/Shutterstock; **p87:** Digoarpi/Shutterstock; **p88(l):** magicinfoto/Shutterstock; **p88(b):** jarvis gray/Shutterstock; **p90-91(bkgd):** Oculo/Shutterstock; **p91(b):** Andy Lidstone/Shutterstock; **p92-93:** colors/Shutterstock; **p99:** EddyCalin/Shutterstock; **p108(bkgd):** Eric Isselee/Shutterstock; **p108(t):** domonabike/Alamy Stock Photo; **p108(m):** Ingo Oeland/Alamy Stock Photo; **p108(t):** Peter Unger/The Image Bank Unreleased/Getty Images; **p109(b):** Tetra Images, LLC/Alamy Stock Photo; **p119:** Marco Tomasini/Shutterstock; **p126(bkgd):** Nmedia/Shutterstock; **p126(tl):** Anastasy Yarmolovich/123RF; **p126(tr):** Errol Rait/Alamy Stock Photo; **p126(mr):** ForsterForest/iStockphoto; **p126(ml):** MJTH/Shutterstock; **p127:** Stephen Simpson/Getty Images; **p128:** Archana bhartia/Shutterstock; **p129(bkgd):** Zerbor/Shutterstock; **p132-133:** koosen/Shutterstock; **p132:** INSADCO Photography/Alamy Stock Photo; **p136:** Kevin Britland/Alamy Stock Photo; **p137(t):** Wonderwall/Shutterstock; **p137(b):** GOLFX/Shutterstock; **p140:** Elena Odareeva/Shutterstock; **p141(t):** Belinda Pretorius/Shutterstock; **p141(b):** Francois van Heerden/Shutterstock; **p142:** Friedrich Stark/Alamy Stock Photo; **p143:** Danita Delimont/Alamy Stock Photo; **p144(bkgd):** Mythja/Shutterstock; **p144(t):** Keren Su/China Span/Alamy Stock Photo; **p144(bl):** E.D. Torial/Alamy Stock Photo; **p144(br):** Jupiterimages/Stockbyte/Getty Images; **p145:** Songquan Deng/Shutterstock; **p146:** Miroslav Kresac/Shutterstock; **p147:** TruNorth Images/Shutterstock; **p150:** Nataly Mayak/Shutterstock; **p152(bkgd):** Donatas1205/Shutterstock; **p152(t):** Guentermanaus/Shutterstock; **p152(b):** Doug Menuez/Forrester Images/Getty Images; **p153:** Jami Tarris/Stone/Getty Images; **p155:** PYMCA/Universal Images Group/Getty Images; **p157:** Vadim Petrakov/Shutterstock.

**Artwork** by Dan Gartman, Vladimir Aleksic, Laura Allen Anderson, Mark Beech, Stefan Chabluk, Katriona Chapman, Chris Coady, Russ Daff, Jacqui Davis, Chiara Fidele, Michael Heath, Carol Liddiment, Lizzie Lissiemore, Francesca Marquez, Gustavo Mazali, Chiara Pasqualotto, Dusan Pavlic, Kate Rochester, Caroline Romanet, Angelika Scudmore, Emma Shaw Smith, Mike Spoor, Katri Valkamo, Nuno Viera, Chris Smedley, Mel Matthews, Meilo So, and Q2A Media Services Pvt. Ltd.

**Michael Morpurgo:** *Kensuke's Kingdom* (Egmont, 1999) copyright © Michael Morpurgo 1999, reprinted by permission of David Higham Associates Ltd for the author.

**Roald Dahl:** *Charlie and the Chocolate Factory,* (Puffin Books, 1973) copyright © Roald Dahl Nominee Ltd, 1964, reprinted by permission of David Higham Associates Ltd for the author.

**Ray Bradbury:** *All Summer in a Day*, first published by Fantasy House (subsidiary of Mercury Press); from March 1958, Mercury Press; since Feb 2001 Van Gelder's Spilogale, Inc, reprinted by permission of Abner Stein for the author.

**Paul Shipton:** *Petey*, Oxford Reading Tree, Treetops Fiction (OUP, 2014). Reproduced with permission of Oxford University Press through PLSclear.

**Paul Shipton:** *Petey* (playscript) adapted by David Calcutt, Oxford Reading Tree, Treetops Playscripts (OUP, 1998). Reproduced with permission of Oxford University Press through PLSclear.

**Jane Clarke:** 'Finding a Friend', first published in *I Wanna be Your Mate* compiled by Tony Bradman (Bloomsbury, 1999), copyright © Jane Clarke 1999. Reprinted with permission of the author.

**Andy Blackford:** Tchang and the Pearl Dragon from *Myths and Legends: Dragon Tales,* Oxford Reading Tree, Treetops, (OUP, 2010). Reproduced with permission of Oxford University Press through PLSclear.

**Elizabeth Laird:** Gelert, The Prince's Hound from *Why Dogs Have Black Noses*, Oxford Reading Tree (OUP, 2010). Reproduced with permission of Oxford University Press through PLSclear.

**Susan Gates:** *The Wooden Horse/Helen of Troy*, Oxford Reading Tree Myths & Legends, (OUP, 2014) copyright © Susan Gates 2010. Reproduced with permission of Oxford University Press through PLSclear.

**Philip Sherlock:** How Crab Got a Hard Back from *Tales from the West Indies* (OUP, 2000) copyright © Philip Sherlock 1966. Reproduced with permission of Oxford University Press through PLSclear.

**Hunter Emigh:** 'Home Country. What's That?' from *Slurping Soup and other confusions: true stories and activities to help third culture kids during transition* by Maryan Afnan Ahmad, Cherie Emigh, Ulrike Gemmer, Barbara Menezes, Kathryn Tonges and Lucinda Willshire, (2e, Summertime Publishing, 2013), www.slurpingsoup.com 2010, copyright © 2010 Slurping Soup and Other Confusions, reprinted with permission of Cherie Emigh.

**Ermine Saner:** Laura Dekker: Sailing solo, *The Guardian* copyright © Guardian News & Media Ltd 2021.

**Emily Dickinson:** 'The Moon was but a Chin of Gold' from *The Poems of Emily Dickinson*, edited by Thomas H. Johnson, Cambridge, Mass.: The Belknap Press of Harvard University Press, Copyright © 1951, 1955 by the President and Fellows of Harvard College. Copyright © renewed 1979, 1983 by the President and Fellows of Harvard College. Copyright © 1914, 1918, 1919, 1924, 1929, 1930, 1932, 1935, 1937, 1942, by Martha Dickinson Bianchi. Copyright © 1952, 1957, 1958, 1963, 1965, by Mary L. Hampson. Reprinted by permission of Harvard University Press.

**Ogden Nash:** The Tale of Custard the Dragon from *Candy is Dandy*, (Welbeck Publishing Group formerly Carlton Books Ltd 1994) copyright © 1936 by Ogden Nash, renewed. Reprinted by permission of Curtis Brown, Ltd and Welbeck Publishing Group.

**Heather Cardwell:** *Abdul in the Souk* copyright © Heather Cardwell (Oxford University Press, 2021). Reprinted with permission of the author.

**Tololwa M Mollel:** *My Rows and Piles of Coins* (Clarion Books, 1999) text copyright © Tololwa M Mollel. Reprinted with permission of Houghton Mifflin Harcourt.

**First News:** web page adapted from 'team' and 'subscribe' pages at www.firstnews.co.uk, by permission of First News.

**Martin Kiszko:** 'Blue Planet's Blue' from *Green Poems for a Blue Planet* (Wild Idea Ltd, 2012) copyright © Martin Kiszko 2010 (www.greenpoemsforablueplanet). Reprinted with permission of the author.

**Tony Mitton:** 'I Wanna Be a Star' from *Plum*, (Scholastic, 1998) copyright © Tony Mitton 1998, reprinted by permission of David Higham Associates Ltd for the author.

Any third-party use of this material, outside of this publication, is prohibited. Interested parties should apply to the copyright holders indicated in each case.

Every effort has been made to contact copyright holders of material reproduced in this book. Any omissions will be rectified in subsequent printings if notice is given to the publisher.

# Contents

In this book you will find stories, poems and facts from these places. We hope you enjoy them!

ARCTIC OCEAN

EUROPE

GREECE

RICA

TANZANIA

IBIA

INDIAN OCEAN

ASIA

CHINA

JAPAN

AUSTRALIA

OCEANIA

NEW ZEALAND

ERN OCEAN

# Unit contents

| Unit | Language, grammar, spelling, vocabulary, phonics | Writing | Speaking and listening |
|---|---|---|---|
| 1 | • Unfamiliar words, definitions<br>• Similes and metaphors<br>• Spelling: words ending -ing, doubling consonants<br>• Using 'but' correctly<br>• Words ending in -er, -or and -ar<br>• Direct speech<br>• Adverbs<br>• Synonyms<br>• Suffixes: words ending -ful and -al | **Fiction**<br>Writing an adventure story | • Ask and answer questions<br>• Talking confidently<br>• Taking on responsibilities |
| 2 | • Commas<br>• Subordinating conjunctions<br>• Modal verbs<br>• Abstract nouns<br>• Specialised non-fiction vocabulary | **Non-fiction**<br>Note taking<br>Non-chronological report writing | • Share personal views and opinions<br>• Questions – develop ideas and extend understanding<br>• Prepare a talk<br>• Organisation of ideas |
| 3 | • Playscript dialogue<br>• Rhymes | **Playscripts and poetry**<br>Note taking<br>Writing poetry<br>Writing a playscript | • Group roles and responsibilities<br>• Portray character through drama<br>• Playscript performance<br>• Group roles |
| **REVISE AND CHECK UNITS 1–3** | | | |
| 4 | • Features of traditional tales and legends<br>• Pronouns<br>• Commas<br>• Apostrophes – possession and contraction<br>• Prepositions<br>• Adverbials | **Fiction**<br>Writing a traditional tale | • Expressing opinions<br>• Use non-verbal communication |
| 5 | • Pronouns<br>• Plurals<br>• Features of biographies<br>• Direct speech<br>• Reported speech<br>• Single-clause and multi-clause sentences<br>• Commas in multi-clause sentences<br>• Features of diaries | **Non-fiction**<br>Writing an autobiography | • Organisation of ideas<br>• Speak for longer periods<br>• Questions – develop ideas and extend understanding |
| 6 | • Personification<br>• Similes and metaphors<br>• Alliteration and onomatopoeia<br>• Subordinating clauses and conjunctions | **Poetry and playscripts**<br>Writing a playscript from a poem | • Confident talking<br>• Expressing opinions<br>• Performance poetry<br>• Group roles and responsibilities<br>• Speak for longer periods<br>• Use non-verbal communication |
| **REVISE AND CHECK UNITS 4–6** | | | |
| 7 | • Unfamiliar words, definitions<br>• Prepositions<br>• Subordinate clauses<br>• Agreement of verbs<br>• Synonyms<br>• Homophones<br>• Spelling strategies | **Fiction**<br>Writing an exciting story | • Expressing opinions<br>• Group roles |
| 8 | • Persuasive language<br>• Opposites and prefixes<br>• Shades of meaning and comparisons<br>• Idioms<br>• Compound words and spelling strategies<br>• Personal pronouns<br>• Possessive pronouns | **Non-fiction**<br>Writing a persuasive advertising campaign<br>Writing a persuasive newspaper article<br>Writing a persuasive letter<br>Writing a persuasive leaflet | • Language choices<br>• Expressing opinions<br>• Group roles<br>• Prepare a talk |
| 9 | • Silent letters<br>• Countable and uncountable nouns | **Poetry**<br>Writing a rap poem | • Performance poetry<br>• Use non-verbal communication<br>• Speak for longer periods<br>• Expressing opinions<br>• Group roles |
| **REVISE AND CHECK UNITS 7–9** | | | |
| **POETRY READING** *The Tale of Custard the Dragon* | | | |

 # A world of adventures!

Arctic Ocean

Atlantic Ocean

Pacific Ocean

Pacific Ocean

Indian Ocean

Southern Ocean

## Talk time

1 Look at the oceans on the map. Water covers nearly three-quarters of the Earth's surface. Which ocean is nearest to the country you live in?

2 What do you think this unit is about? How do you know?

3 Have you seen a storm at sea or on land? If so, tell a partner about it.

"I'm not afraid of storms for I'm learning how to sail my ship."
Louisa May Alcott

# Describing the sea

- Ask and answer questions
- Use a dictionary to find the meaning of words
- Recognise synonyms

On this page you will learn some exciting verbs that help you to imagine storms at sea. Verbs are 'doing words' so they tell you what the sea **does**. *Example:* The sea **roars** and **pounds** on the beach.

**A**  Copy the words below and match each word to its meaning. Use a dictionary to help you. The first one has been done for you.

| | | | |
|---|---|---|---|
| **1** | crashing | **a** | moving in a curve |
| **2** | curling | **b** | beating down |
| **3** | exploding | **c** | making a loud noise |
| **4** | lashing | **d** | moving like a whip |
| **5** | pounding | **e** | moving something quickly up and down or sideways |
| **6** | shaking | **f** | falling |
| **7** | tumbling | **g** | bursting with a loud bang |

Because there is so much water on Earth, it is sometimes called 'The Blue Planet'.

**B**  Rewrite the sentences below. Change the words that are underlined with words from the list. The first one has been done for you.

> vast   din   awestruck   fearsome   battering

1  The boy watched the **vast** waves.
2  The sea was <u>hitting</u> the ship.
3  He was <u>amazed</u> by the scene.
4  He heard the <u>noise</u> of the water crashing against the boat.
5  A <u>scary</u> creature appeared out of nowhere.

**With a partner, discuss which sentences sound more interesting – those with the underlined words or the new ones you have written.**

- Read a story by a well-known author

## An adventure story

Michael has been sailing around the world with his parents in a boat called the *Peggy Sue*. In a fierce storm, Michael and his dog Stella were washed into the sea. They are now on a **remote** desert island but it seems that they are not alone; someone keeps leaving them food.

**Glossary**

**remote** far from anywhere else

**awestruck** filled with wonder

**typhoon** very strong storm at sea

**witnessing** watching

### Storm at Sea

A storm broke over the island that night, such a fearsome storm, such a thunderous crashing of lightning overhead, such a din of rain and wind that sleep was quite impossible. Great waves roared in from the ocean, pounding the beach, and shaking the ground beneath me.
5 I spread out my sleeping mat at the very back of the cave…

It was fully four days before the storm blew itself out, but even during the worst of it, I would find my fish and fruit breakfast waiting for me every morning. Stella and I kept to the shelter of our cave. All we could do was watch as the rain came lashing down outside. I looked on
10 **awestruck** at the power of the vast waves rolling in from the open sea, curling, tumbling, and exploding as they broke onto the beach, as if they were trying to batter the island into pieces and then suck us all out to sea. I thought often of my mother and father and the *Peggy Sue*, and wondered where they were.
15 I just hoped the **typhoon** – for that was what I was **witnessing** – had passed them by.

From *Kensuke's Kingdom* by Michael Morpurgo

# Comprehension

**A** Write answers to these questions, using the extract to help you.

1 When did the storm break out?

2 Who was with Michael on the island?

3 How long did the storm last?

4 What did Michael have to eat?

**B** Write answers to these questions, using the extract to help you.

1 Why does Michael stay inside the cave?

2 Why couldn't Michael fall asleep?

3 Michael thought about his parents. Where do you think they were?

4 Look at how the writer describes the waves in lines 10 to 12. What sort of picture does it create in the reader's mind?

**C** 1 Read the story again, then retell it to a partner using your own words. Use powerful words to create a dramatic picture. List these words to use in your own writing.

2 What is the first thing you would do if you found yourself on a remote island? Explain your ideas to your partner.

- Explain the writer's choice of language
- Find information and use clues in the story to answer questions
- List powerful vocabulary to use in your own work

**?**

How would you feel if you were caught in a typhoon, or another type of dramatic weather? Would you be excited or frightened or both? Explain your answer carefully.

# Similes and metaphors

- Recognise similes and metaphors
- Use similes and metaphors in your speech and writing

Writers use **similes** and **metaphors** to create comparisons in the reader's mind. A **simile** always uses the words **like** or **as**. A **metaphor** says something *is* something else.

*Examples:* He is **like** a bright light. (simile)
He **is** the bright light of the school. (metaphor)

**A** Read the sentences below. With a partner, decide which comparisons are similes and which are metaphors.

   **a** The waves pounded like a drum on the shore.
   **b** The teeth of crocodiles are white daggers.
   **c** The fog enveloped us like a thick, grey duvet.
   **d** Life is an ocean with its ups and downs.
   **e** The room was as untidy as the inside of the school wastepaper bin.

**B** Copy and complete the similes below using your own ideas.

   **a** The night was as dark as _____ .
   **b** Like _____ , the aeroplane rose in the air.
   **c** The sea was as angry as _____ .
   **d** Her legs shook like _____ .
   **e** The storm arrived like _____ .

**Stretch zone**

Create a list of interesting similes and metaphors that you find in the books you read. It could be made into a display for the classroom.

**C** Write a paragraph about a storm – either on land or at sea. Include the storm beginning, then getting worse and gradually dying out. Use **at least** two similes and two metaphors.

# Spelling rules: words ending -ing

There are rules for adding the suffix **-ing** to a word.

● Most words just add **-ing** to the root word.
*Examples:* happen**ing**, pay**ing**, pour**ing**

● If the root word ends in **-e**, take off the **e** and add **-ing**.
*Examples:* take - tak**ing**, create - creat**ing**

● If the root word ends in a short vowel sound then a
consonant, double the last letter then add **-ing**.
*Examples:* get - gett**ing**, put - putt**ing**

**A** Copy and complete the table below.

| Root word | *-ing* added |
|-----------|--------------|
| break     |              |
|           | hoping       |
| roll      |              |
|           | crashing     |
| rumble    |              |
|           | exploding    |
| run       |              |

**B** Read the paragraph below. Find five words ending -ing with
incorrect spelling. Write the correct spelling of each word.

I was runing so quickly that everything was droping out
of my rucksack. I only had half an hour left to get to the
rideing stables to get ready for the race. Would we make
a wining team? I knew that as soon as I saw my horse
I would be huging him – just for luck.

**C** 1 Using the spelling rules, add **-ing** to each of these verbs.

use add make forget help dig wear carry lap tumble

2 Put the words into these spelling rule groups.

| Add -ing | Drop -e and add -ing | Double the last letter and add -ing |
|----------|----------------------|-------------------------------------|
|          |                      |                                     |

3 Choose two words from each column and write a sentence
for each of them.

- Write multi-clause sentences using the conjunction 'but'

# Using 'but' correctly

The conjunction **but** is often used to show contrast with the first clause. *Example:* In *Kensuke's Kingdom*, Michael Morpurgo writes: 'It was fully four days before the storm blew itself out, but even during the worst of it, I would find my fish and fruit basket waiting…'

**A** Copy and complete the sentences by adding a contrast that would not be expected from the first clause.

1 I wanted to swim in the sea, but…

2 Johan was very nervous about going out in a boat, but…

3 Tchai lost his school bag, but…

4 She is a great swimmer, but…

**B** In six of the sentences below, the conjunction **but** should have been used instead of **and** to link contrasting clauses. Which ones are they? Correct and write out the six sentences.

1 The forecast was for rain and it stayed sunny all day.

2 Mohammed sent in his application for the team and waited for an answer.

3 He was tired and kept working.

4 The rained poured down and the storm raged on.

5 He is rich and he is not happy.

6 Charlotte wanted to take her boat out and she wasn't experienced to sail it on her own.

7 We ordered strawberry ice cream and received vanilla.

8 She bought him a shirt and he hated the colour.

**C** Write three sentences of your own using **but** to introduce a contrasting clause. Remember to use a comma before **but**!

**Language tip**
A comma before **but** means that the second clause is a contrasting idea.

**Stretch zone**

Find examples of the writer using the word **but** in a book you are reading. Is it always used to show a contrast? If not, how else is it used?

# Spelling rules: words ending -er, -or and -ar

The endings **-er**, **-or**, and **-ar** can be confused. Remember:

● **-er** and **-or** endings make nouns which describe someone who performs the action of a verb.
*Examples:* teach/teach**er**, garden/garden**er**

● **-er** endings are most common.

● **-or** is often used for technical and professional nouns.
*Examples:* solicit**or**, profess**or**

● words ending **-ar** can be nouns or adjectives.
*Examples:* doll**ar** (noun), circul**ar** (adjective)

**A** Add -**er** or -**or** to the word roots below to make a noun.
Use a dictionary to help you.

**a** govern____          **d** protest____

**b** bak____             **e** dressmak____

**c** edit____            **f** act____

**B** Add -**ar** to the examples below to make four nouns and four adjectives. Then copy and complete the table.

**a** cell____            **d** peculi____

**b** simil____           **e** caterpill____

**c** calend____          **f** particul____

| Noun | Adjective |
| --- | --- |
|  |  |
|  |  |
|  |  |

**C** **1** Make the following verbs into nouns by adding -**er**, -**or** or -**ar**.

**a** plan          **b** beg          **c** travel

What else did you need to change in these words?

**2** Make these verbs into nouns by adding -**er**, -**or** or -**ar**.

**a** refrigerate   **b** calculate   **c** lie

What else did you need to change in these words?

- Read a story by a well-known author

# Chocolate fantasy fiction

Charlie Bucket doesn't usually have any money and he is always hungry. He would love to win a golden ticket to visit the famous Willy Wonka's chocolate factory. One day, he finds a fifty pence coin.

## Glossary

**fifty pence/five-penny pieces** UK money

**bulged** swelled

**sonny** friendly name for a boy

**change** the money returned after buying something

**wolfing** eating greedily

**extraordinarily** unusually

## The Miracle

Charlie entered the shop and laid the damp **fifty pence** on the counter.

"One Wonka's Whipple-Scrumptious Fudgemallow Delight," he said, remembering how much he had loved the one he
5 had on his birthday.

The man behind the counter looked fat and well-fed. He had big lips and fat cheeks and a very fat neck. The fat around his neck **bulged** out all around the top of his collar like a rubber ring. He turned and reached behind
10 him for the chocolate bar, then he turned back again and handed it to Charlie. Charlie grabbed it and quickly tore off the wrapper and took an enormous bite. Then he took another… and another… and oh, the joy of being able to fill one's mouth with rich
15 solid food!

"You look like you wanted that one, **sonny**," the shopkeeper said pleasantly.

Charlie nodded, his mouth bulging with chocolate.

The shopkeeper put Charlie's **change** on the counter.
20 "Take it easy," he said. "It'll give you a tummy ache if you swallow it like that without chewing."

Charlie went on **wolfing** the chocolate. He couldn't stop. And in less than half a minute, the whole thing had disappeared down his throat. He was quite out of breath, but
25 he felt marvellously, **extraordinarily**, happy. He reached out a hand to take the change. Then he paused. His eyes were just above the level of the counter. They were staring at the silver coins lying there. The coins were all **five-penny pieces**. There were nine of them altogether. Surely it wouldn't matter if he
30 spent just one more…

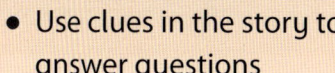

- Use clues in the story to answer questions
- Predict what might happen next

"I think," he said quietly, "I think… I'll have just one more of those chocolate bars. The same kind as before, please."

"Why not?" the fat shopkeeper said, reaching behind him
35 again and taking another Whipple-Scrumptious Fudgemallow Delight from the shelf. He laid it on the counter.

Charlie picked it up and tore off the wrapper… and *suddenly*… from underneath the wrapper… there came a flash of gold.

Charlie's heart stood still.

40 "It's a Golden Ticket!" screamed the shopkeeper, leaping about a foot in the air. "You've got a Golden Ticket!"

From *Charlie and the Chocolate Factory* by Roald Dahl

# Comprehension

**A** Write answers to these questions, using the extract to help you.

1 What was Charlie's favourite sweet called?

2 How did Charlie feel when he had swallowed the chocolate bar?

3 What did Charlie decide to do instead of taking his change?

4 What does Charlie see when he opens the second chocolate bar?

**B** Discuss the answers to these questions with a partner. Find quotes from the story to support your answer.

1 How do we know that Charlie doesn't have chocolate very often?

2 What is Charlie's reaction when he finds the golden ticket?

3 What do you think will happen next in the story?

**C** Write a short paragraph describing how you think Charlie felt when he found the Golden Ticket.

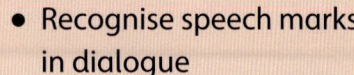

- Recognise speech marks in dialogue
- Know how to punctuate speech correctly

# Direct speech

- Speech marks (" ") go before and after words spoken in a text.
  *Example:* **"**Here's your change, sonny**,"** the shopkeeper said.
- A new line starts every time a new person speaks.
  *Example:* **"**What would you like, sonny?**"** asked the shopkeeper.
  **"**I'll have two chocolate bars, please,**"** said Charlie.
- A capital letter is used for the opening word of a speech.
- A comma is used before the speech marks close.
  *Example:* "I feel marvellously happy**,**" said Charlie.
- Question marks and exclamation marks go **inside** the speech marks.
  *Examples:* "What would you like**?**" asked the shopkeeper.
  "He's won**!**" the man shouted.
- The reporting clause, that tells us who is talking, can come at the start, middle or end of the sentence.
  *Example:* "Take it easy," **he said**, "it'll give you a tummy ache." (middle)

**A** Rewrite the sentences below. Add speech marks and punctuation in the correct places.

  **1** The boy said He's won the golden ticket.

  **2** Do you know where Mr Wonka's factory is I said.

  **3** I'm not sure which way to go said Charlie.

  **4** You'll get a sore tummy if you eat it all at once said Mr Wonka.

**B** Rewrite the sentences above so that **said** is in a different place.

  *Example:* "He's won the golden ticket!" **the boy said.**

**C** Rewrite the text below, changing each word 'said' to one of the words in the list. Add the correct punctuation.

  > shouted    screamed    asked    exclaimed

  Charlie picked up the chocolate bar and tore off the wrapper… and suddenly there came a flash of gold. What is that <u>said</u> the shopkeeper I think it's a Golden Ticket, to visit Mr Wonka's chocolate factory <u>said</u> Charlie Hey, <u>said</u> the shopkeeper Would you believe it, you've won he <u>said</u>.

**Stretch zone**

With a partner, write your own dialogue, set in a sweet shop with two characters talking. Practise speaking your dialogue with your partner.

- Know that adverbs describe actions
- Use adverbs in sentences

# Adverbs

An **adverb** gives more information about a verb. It tells you how, when or where the verb happens.

*Examples:*

How? The student answered **politely**.

When? She played the piano **today**.

Where? The teachers are talking **downstairs**.

Many 'how' adverbs put **-ly** on the end of an adjective.

*Example:* Charlie quick**ly** tore off the chocolate wrapper.

**Rule** When an adjective ends in the letter **y**, change the **y** to an **i** and then add **-ly** to turn it into an adverb.

*Example:* nois**y**/nois**ily**

**A** Change these adjectives into adverbs by adding -ly. Remember the rule.

> lazy   silent   happy   scary   marvellous

**B** In pairs, copy the list of adverbs below. Beside each adverb, write whether it is telling you **how**, **where** or **when** something happened. The first one has been done for you.

**1** outside – where

**2** tomorrow

**3** cheerfully

**4** yesterday

**5** quickly

**6** somewhere

**7** before

**8** lazily

**Language tip**

Remember, an adjective describes a noun. An adverb describes a verb.

**C** Adverbs are useful in speech (dialogue) because they tell us how a person speaks. Write six separate dialogue sentences of your own. Use a different adverb from the list below for each sentence to describe how the person speaks.

> slowly   kindly   rudely   furiously
> anxiously   cheerfully   suddenly

*Example:* "Don't move," she said **slowly**. "I think there's somebody in the house."

● Read a science fiction story

# Future worlds: life on Venus

Imagine living on a planet where rain falls all the time, except for one day every seven years – when the sun comes out for one hour. That's what it's like on the planet Venus, in this story, where the children of settlers from Earth have grown up. The story takes place on that one day.

## Glossary

**jungle** a thick, tangled forest
**released** let go
**tumultuously** in a confused, excited way
**resilient** able to go back into shape
**suspended** held
**savoured** enjoyed

### All Summer in a Day

The sun came out.

It was the colour of flaming bronze and it was very large. And the sky around it was a blazing blue tile colour. And the **jungle** burned with sunlight as the children, **released** from their spell,
5  rushed out, yelling, into the summertime.

"Now, don't go too far," called the teacher after them. "You've only one hour, you know. You wouldn't want to get caught out!"

But they were running and turning their faces up to the sky and feeling the sun on their cheeks like a warm iron; they were
10  taking off their jackets and letting the sun burn their arms.

"Oh, it's better than the sunlamps, isn't it?"

"Much, much better!"

They stopped running and stood in the great jungle that covered Venus, that grew and never
15  stopped growing, **tumultuously**, even as you watched it. It was the colour of rubber and ash, this jungle from the many years without sun. It was the colour of stones and white cheeses and ink.

20  The children lay out, laughing, on the jungle mattress, and heard it sigh and squeak under them, **resilient** and alive.
They ran among the trees, they slipped and fell, they pushed each other, they played hide-
25  and-seek and tag but most of all they squinted at the sun until tears ran down their faces, they put their hands up at that yellowness and that amazing blueness and they breathed of the fresh fresh air and listened and listened to the silence which **suspended** them in a blessed

- Find information from the story to answer questions
- Explain the writer's choice of language
- Describe the characters' thoughts and feelings

30 sea of no sound and no motion. They looked at everything and **savoured** everything. Then, wildly, like animals escaped from their caves, they ran and ran in shouting circles. They ran for an hour and did not stop running.

And then —

35 In the midst of their running, one of the girls wailed.

Everyone stopped.

The girl, standing in the open, held out her hand.

"Oh, look, look," she said trembling.

They came slowly to look at her opened palm. In the
40 centre of it, cupped and huge, was a single raindrop.

From *Science Fiction Stories* by Ray Bradbury

# Comprehension

**A**   Use the story to help you find answers to these questions. Write your answers in complete sentences.

    **1**   Why did the children rush outside?

    **2**   How did the children normally get their sunshine?

    **3**   Why was the jungle the colour of rubber and ash?

**B**   Discuss these questions with a partner.

    **1**   Why does the writer describe the one hour of sunshine as 'summertime'?

    **2**   Find a phrase the writer uses to describe the jungle. What do you think the writer is trying to help the reader to understand by using this phrase?

**C**   Write two more paragraphs to continue the story. Explain how the children feel when the rain returns and they have to go back inside.

 **Stretch zone**

Science fiction stories are set in the future. With a partner, discuss why you think science fiction stories are so popular.

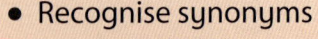

- Recognise synonyms
- Order synonyms according to their strength
- Use synonyms to make sentences more interesting

# Synonyms

A thesaurus is a book of **synonyms** – words which have almost the same meaning.

*Example:* If you looked up **thin**, you would find words such as **slim**, **slender**, **slight**, **skinny** and **lean**. There will also be the antonym (opposite) of thin: **fat**.

**A** Unscramble the words below. Find three synonyms for the word **hot** and three synonyms for the word **cold**.

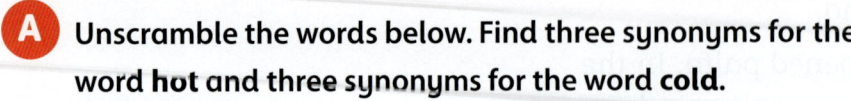

| bolingi | scrochnig | frsoty | ciy | sweeltirng | rozefn |

**B** These three synonyms for **hot** have been put in order from the least hot to the hottest:

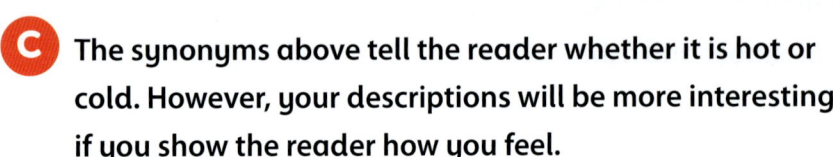

| balmy | humid | sizzling |

**1** Use a thesaurus to make a list of ten synonyms for **cold**. Then put them in order from the least cold to the coldest. Compare your list with a partner.

**2** Write five sentences that each use a different synonym from activity B1.

**C** The synonyms above tell the reader whether it is hot or cold. However, your descriptions will be more interesting if you show the reader how you feel.

*Example:*

'I felt cold.' – this simply tells the reader a fact.

'I dug my fingers deeper into my pockets, desperately seeking warmth.' – this description shows how you felt and what you did.

**Write four descriptive sentences showing the reader that you are feeling:**

**a** hot

**b** hungry

**c** happy

**d** excited.

**Stretch zone**

Look at a chapter in a story you are reading. Write as many synonyms for the word **said** as you can find in your story. See who can find the most.

# Spelling rules: words ending -ful and -al

- You can add the suffix **-ful** to the end of a noun to change it to an adjective.
  *Example:* help/help**ful**
- When a noun ends with **y**, change the **y** into **i** before adding the suffix.
  *Example:* beaut**y**/beaut**i**ful
- You can use the suffix **-al** to change a verb to a noun.
  *Example:* approve/approv**al**
- When a verb ends in an **e**, remove the **e** before adding the suffix **-al**.

- Know the spelling rules for adding the suffixes -ful and -al
- Know the rules for suffixes beginning with vowels and with consonants

**A** Rewrite the sentences below. Fill the gaps using one of the listed words as an adjective ending **-ful**. Use each word only once.

> peace   wonder   duty   plenty

1 The tree gave us a _____ supply of juicy apples.
2 My grandparents tell me to be a _____ son and help with the chores and study hard.
3 Our class had a _____ hour outside in the Venus sun.
4 The lunch area was quiet and _____ today.

**B** With a partner, add the suffix **-ful** to the words below. Choose five of these words and write five sentences using these words.

> thought   tear   help   thank   waste   rest   pain

*Example:* We had a **restful** holiday by the sea last year.

**C** 1 Add the suffix **-al** to these words, remembering the 'e' spelling rule.

> survive   remove   arrive

2 Write pairs of sentences for each word. The first sentence should use the word as a verb. The second sentence should use the word as a noun.

**Stretch zone**

With a partner, write a list of as many words as you can ending **-ful** and **-al**. Then test each other on the spelling and meaning of the words. Use a dictionary to help you.

- Plan a story
- Create suspense

# Write an adventure story

You are going to write an adventure story about a sea rescue.

Most good adventures have:

- a setting (where and when it happens)
- characters (the people in the story)
- a problem (something that goes wrong)
- suspense (which makes the reader want to find out what happens next)
- a resolution (which tells you how the problem was solved).

**1**  YOU are the main character! Imagine walking by the sea one day. You see someone in the sea… Use a writing frame like the one below to plan your own short story about an adventure and rescue at sea, but use your own ideas too. Write your plan in note form and use the headings below.

| Questions to think about | Useful phrases |
|---|---|
| **Setting** | |
| Where and when did it happen? | It was… |
| **Characters** | |
| Who did you see in the sea? | All of a sudden / To my surprise / To my horror |
| | I saw / noticed / heard |
| What was he / she doing? | He / She was waving / shouting / holding a rope |
| What did the person look like? | He / She had grey hair / a yellow jacket / a blue hat |
| **Problem** | |
| Where was the person? | near / far from / way out |
| | a boat / the shore / the rocks |
| Why did the person need help? | no life jacket / a long way out / couldn't swim |
| **Suspense** | |
| What were the dangers? | tide coming in / a shark approaching / boat drifting |
| Why was it difficult for you? | no life jacket / no mobile phone / no boat |
| **Resolution** | |
| How did you rescue him / her? | Suddenly I remembered / noticed / realised… |
| | At last / Eventually / To my relief… |

## 1N Fiction Writing workshop

- Use imaginative vocabulary to describe setting and characters
- Proof-read each other's work

**2** Now you can begin writing your story. The frame below gives you some ideas, but you can use your own if you prefer.

| | |
|---|---|
| It was a… | Sunday morning in December.<br>cool evening in March.<br>lazy afternoon in July. |
| I was walking… | beside the rocks on my way to…<br>near the beach because…<br>along the cliff to find… |
| The sea was… | sparkling in the sun.<br>crashing against the rocks. |
| The lapping waves…<br>The tumbling waves… | sounded like… |

**Language tip**

Remember the similes and metaphors from page 12? Use some in your writing to help your reader imagine the scene you're describing.

**3** Check your partner's writing for errors. Comment on the way they have described the scene.

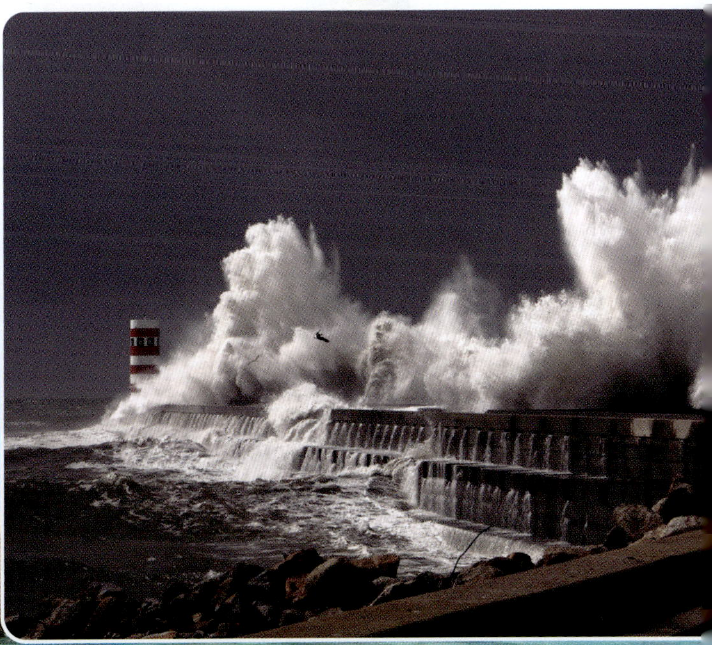

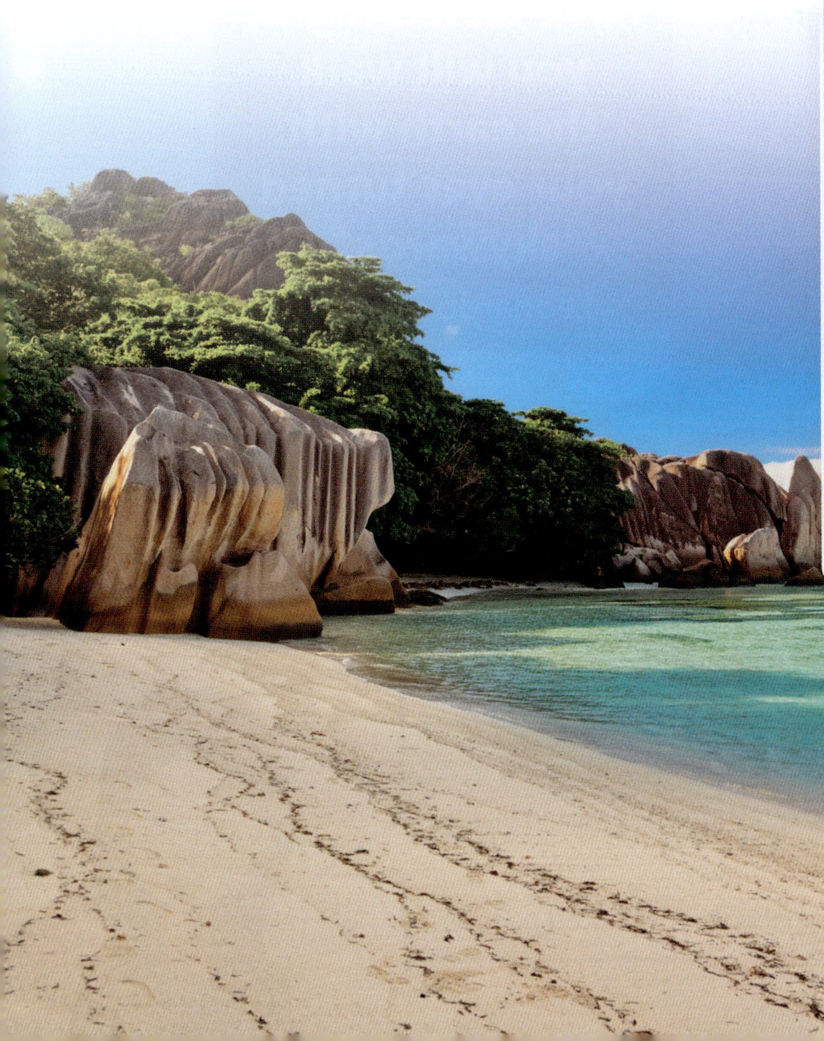

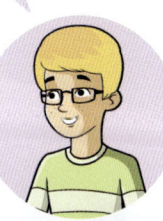

# 2 Travels far and wide

A

B

C

D

> "For once you have tasted flight, you will walk the earth with your eyes turned skywards."
>
> Leonardo da Vinci

## Talk time

1 These four pictures show different flight inventions. Which one do you know least about? Think of two questions you would like to find the answers to.

2 Why do you think the idea of flying has always fascinated people?

- Ask questions to help you understand
- Share ideas and explain your opinions
- Give a short talk

**A** Match the captions below to the pictures on page 26.

1 A model of Leonardo da Vinci's ornithopter (flying machine)

2 The space shuttle is launched by two rocket boosters

3 A birdman flies in his super lightweight wingsuit

4 The Boeing *Dreamliner* is so light it uses less fuel than a normal aircraft

**B** Read the notes below and prepare a short talk for the class about the ornithopter.

- Leonardo da Vinci born in Vinci, Italy, 1452
- Famous artist and inventor
- Fascinated by how birds flew
- Wanted to invent a machine to help humans fly
- Designed the ORNITHOPTER – which flapped its wings like a bird
- Only drew it – never built it
- Recently, Todd Reichart built an ornithopter based on da Vinci's drawing. It flew 145 metres

**Stretch zone**

Which way of travelling do you think is the best: on land, through the air or by sea? Give reasons for your choice.

**C** How have aeroplanes and air travel made a difference to the world? Think of two good and two bad points. Use some of these words to help you explain your ideas to a partner.

speed   explore   visit   pollution   noise
business   holidays   airports

The first successful flight of a powered aeroplane was by the Wright brothers in 1903.

# Life in the sea

Life on Earth began in the sea millions of years ago. As time passed, thousands of different sea plants and animals took on many shapes, sizes and colours. Some began to swim, some began to crawl. Some are still
5  around today and some are not.

### Dead and gone

Trilobites were some of the earliest animals. They lived in the sea more than 510 million years ago. They had jointed legs and hard shells like crabs. We don't know
10  why, but about 250 million years ago they all died out, so trilobites became **extinct**. We only know about trilobites because some of their remains turned into stones called **fossils**. Scientists use the fossils to work out how long ago trilobites and other animals lived.

15  ### Still here today

The brittle star is a sea creature that is luckier than the trilobite! This 180-million-year-old fossil looks like brittle stars that are still alive today. Brittle stars have a round central disc and five arms that can easily break. Large numbers of them can be
20  found these days on sandy or muddy sea beds.

### Why do some animals become extinct?

So why did the trilobite become extinct and why did the brittle star **survive**? After all, the trilobites lived on Earth for about 270 million years. Is it because something
25  happened to their food chain?

### Food chains

The diagram on the right shows how a simple food chain works.

In this food chain, if all the grass died, the rabbits might die
30  out too, because they would have no food. This would cause a problem for the foxes, who eat animals like rabbits. Thinking back to the trilobites, scientists tell us that many other kinds of plants and animals became extinct at the same time as the trilobites. Perhaps trilobites died out because something
35  happened to destroy their food chain.

**Glossary**

**extinct** no longer alive
**fossils** hardened remains of plants or animals
**survive** continue to live
**herbivore** plant eater
**carnivore** meat eater

A trilobite

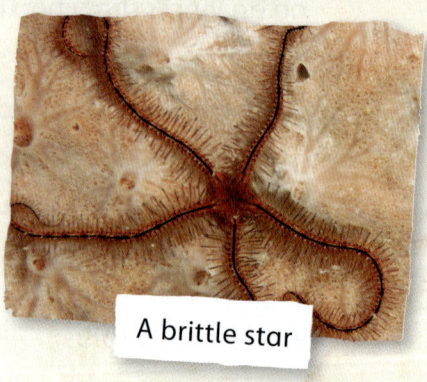

A brittle star

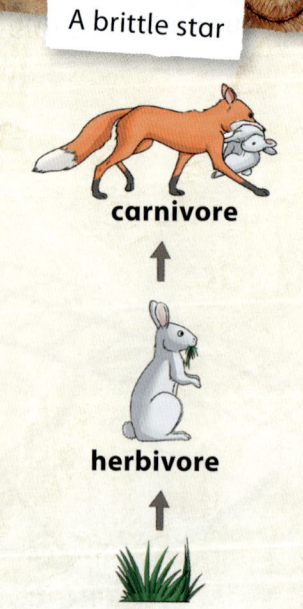

**carnivore**

**herbivore**

**grass**

Simple food chain

# Comprehension

- Identify the most important ideas in a text
- Find the answers to questions
- Use words linked to the topic

**A** Write short answers to the following questions.

1 Name two physical features of a trilobite.

2 Name an animal that lived more than a million years ago and can still be found today.

3 How long did trilobites live on the Earth for?

4 What happens to the animals in a food chain if the plants die?

**B** Choose the correct word in each sentence.

1 Life in the sea began **thousands/millions** of years ago.

2 Fossils are the remains of plants or animals in **stone/mud**.

3 Animals that are extinct are no longer **alive/eating**.

4 An animal that eats plants is a **carnivore/herbivore**.

**C** 1 What is the main point of each of the five paragraphs in the extract? Write five sentences, explaining the main point of each paragraph.

2 Where do you think humans fit into the marine (sea) food chain? Explain your answer by drawing a diagram.

**Stretch zone**

How might humans be responsible for the extinction of sea plants and animals? Talk about your ideas with a partner.

# Commas

- Use commas to separate subordinate clauses from main clauses
- Use commas to separate clauses in the middle of sentences

**Commas** are used to separate words, phrases and clauses to make the meaning clearer.

**A** In the non-fiction text *Life in the sea*, the writer has used commas in different ways.

Find and write out a sentence that shows a comma used:

**1** before the conjunction **but**

**2** before a clause beginning with **if**

**3** after a clause beginning with **As**.

**Language tip**
Remember that a clause is a group of words that contains a verb. Phrases do not always contain a verb.

**B** Four commas have been left out of the extract below.
Copy out the extract, putting the commas in the right places.

I like to travel and visit lots of cities but I don't like flying. If I could travel thousands of miles by car then I would drive all the way. As an experienced traveller I know I have to fly to get to distant places. Tomorrow I will overcome my fears and book a flight to Alaska.

**Pairs of commas** can separate a clause or phrase in the middle of a sentence.

*Example:* The waves**,** which were the biggest I had ever seen**,** rolled over the town.

**C** Rewrite the sentences below. Put the clauses in brackets into the middle of the sentences. The first one has been done for you.

**1** Rabbits are herbivores. (who eat grass)
Rabbits, who eat grass, are herbivores.

**2** The brittle star is still found in sea beds today. (which is a sea creature)

**3** Fossils can tell us about the earliest animals on our planet. (which are hardened remains)

**Stretch zone**

Think about the different ways commas can be used. Write a few sentences using commas in different ways.

# Subordinating conjunctions

- Recognise subordinating conjunctions
- Write multi-clause sentences using subordinating conjunctions

**Subordinating conjunctions** link a main clause and a subordinate clause. A main clause works on its own but a subordinate clause doesn't.

*Example:*

subordinating conjunction

I like to have a window seat if I fly on an aeroplane.

main clause      subordinating clause

Subordinating conjunctions, such as **because**, **so**, **as** and **if**, are important because they link and explain points precisely.

**A**   **Rewrite the sentences below. Circle the subordinating conjunctions and underline the subordinate clauses. The first one has been done for you.**

1   Some animals do not survive (because) they don't have enough food.

2   We can find out about extinct animals and plants if we study fossils.

3   The food chain is explained in a diagram so it is easy to understand.

4   Brittle stars still exist today, as the report explains.

**B**   **With a partner, decide which of the subordinating conjunctions listed below is the best one to complete each sentence.**

> if    because    while    before

1   I am going to look for fossils _____ it starts to rain.

2   I will draw a diagram _____ it will help to explain my ideas.

3   I like to listen to music _____ I am reading.

4   You can come too, _____ you promise to behave.

**C**   **Rewrite the sentences below, adding a subordinate clause using one of these conjunctions.**

> so    because    if    as    when    after    before

1   We will go to the airport.

2   The woman flew in the space shuttle.

3   Some animals are carnivores.

4   Some sea creatures died out.

- Read a non-chronological report

# It's all hot air

The first hot air balloon passengers were a sheep, a duck and a **cockerel**! In 1783 they travelled for seven minutes in a balloon built by Frenchmen Joseph and Étienne Montgolfier.

### 5 How hot air balloons work

Hot air is lighter than cool air, so a balloon rises when the air inside it is heated. Modern hot air balloons have gas burners which heat the air inside the **balloon's envelope**. A balloon will go higher or lower depending on how much 10 gas is burned.

### Flying hot air balloons

Some people have balloons for fun while others enter competitions in them. Large pleasure balloons carry passengers who pay for the flight. It is even possible to fly 15 over the Egyptian pyramids in a balloon. While the balloon is up, somebody follows it with a car and trailer, ready to collect the people and equipment on landing. They are in touch with the crew by radio.

Balloon pilots navigate with a map, which is often on a 20 laptop. They also have a **GPS**, so that they know where they are. An altimeter tells them how high they are.

### How modern hot air balloons are made

The balloon's envelope is made of very strong **nylon**. The bottom part of the 25 envelope is made of 'Nomex', a fabric which cannot catch fire. Steel **cables** attach the basket and burners to the balloon's envelope.

**Glossary**

**cockerel** male chicken

**balloon's envelope** the fabric part of the balloon that fills with hot air

**GPS** global positioning system, which uses satellites to find the position of a vehicle or a person

**nylon** very strong, man-made material

**cables** thick metal wires

Balloons are sometimes used for advertising.

envelope

skirt

burners

wicker basket

# Comprehension

**A** Write short answers to the following questions. Compare your answers with a partner's.

1 What passengers travelled for seven minutes in 1783?

2 What makes a hot air balloon go higher?

3 How is the air inside a hot air balloon's envelope heated?

4 Why can't modern hot air balloons catch fire?

**B** Work with a partner to answer these questions.

1 What is the purpose of the non-chronological report *It's all hot air*? Which two statements below are correct?

  **a** To explain how hot air balloons work

  **b** To persuade the reader to go on a hot air balloon trip

  **c** To inform the reader about hot air balloons

  **d** To argue that hot air balloons are important

2 What is the purpose of the subheadings?

3 Choose one paragraph that you think is very clear. Change it into a drawing or diagram to explain the topic clearly to someone else. Don't forget to add labels.

**C** Plan and write a step-by-step route for a hot air balloon trip. The route will be above your own town, city or province and needs to be of interest to those flying in the balloon. The car and trailer have to follow the balloon's route on the ground.

*Example:* START: take off on the school sports field

First place of interest is the botanic gardens and wildlife park...

**Stretch zone**

Why do you think people use hot air balloons to advertise things?

# Modal verbs

The most common modal verbs are: **will**, **would**, **should**, **can**, **could**, **may**, **might**, **must**, **shall**, **ought to**.

They are always used with another verb.

Modal verbs show the possibility or certainty of something happening.

*Examples:* We **might** play football today.

We **will** play football today.

**Will** means playing football is certain but **might** means it is only a possibility.

**A** Complete these sentences with ideas of your own.

1 If I go travelling, I might...

2 If I went travelling, I could...

3 If I went travelling, I would...

4 If I go travelling, I must...

**B** Rewrite these sentences and put suitable modal verbs in the gaps. Don't use the same modal verb twice.

1 Look, I _____ see the hot air balloon in the sky!

2 Before the balloon takes off, the envelope _____ be filled up with hot air.

3 The basket _____ not be as strong without the steel cables.

4 You _____ be careful with the burners because they are very hot.

5 You _____ take care when climbing into the basket.

**C** Write four sentences showing different chances of you being able to go on a flight in a hot air balloon, such as, *I shall fly in a hot air balloon on my birthday*. Write out your sentences in the order of possibility, beginning with the least likely.

> • Know that abstract nouns can't be seen, touched or heard
> • Recognise and use abstract nouns

# Abstract nouns

> **Abstract nouns** are nouns that you can't see, hear, touch, taste or smell.
>
> *Examples:* intelligence, bravery, Friday, summer, friendship, anger.

**A** With a partner, find the abstract nouns from the list of words below and write them down.

> happiness   flowers   pain   playground   kindness
> April   freedom   education   people   evening
> stars  skill   truth   pleasure   balloon   imagination
> morning   glass   shock   childhood

**B** Rewrite the sentences below and add a suitable abstract noun from the list you wrote in activity A.

1 I caught the aeroplane early in the _____.

2 The pilot said, "It's a _____ to fly you today."

3 He went on holiday in _____.

4 I had a _____ when a man in a wingsuit landed in my garden!

5 Aeroplanes give people the _____ to travel to different countries.

**C** Make up five sentences of your own using each of the abstract nouns below. If you need ideas, use the pictures on this page.

> luxury   courage   adventure   friendship   dream

• Read an information text

# The origins of Chocolate

Chocolate is made from **cacao**. The **Maya** of Mexico discovered cacao as long ago as 600 **CE**. They picked cacao from the wild trees and then began to plant cacao trees specially.

5 The **Aztec** people became powerful after the Maya. They were very fond of chocolatl, a drink made from roasted cacao beans and water with hot chilli to make it spicy.

## Precious beans

10 Cacao beans were so valuable that they were used as money. A rabbit cost ten beans and a pumpkin cost four. They were also used in important ceremonies and traded for cloth, **jade** and ceremonial feathers.

A cacao tree produces between 20 and 30 pods a year.
15 Pods from one tree would make 450 grams of chocolate powder, about the same weight as a small bag of sugar. There are about 20 to 40 beans in each pod.

## Powder to bars

Soon people began to add milk to the chocolate, but it
20 was still only a drink. Then, from about 1850, factories began to **manufacture** and sell cocoa powder in tins and this led to chocolate bars. Mexican women used to press cocoa powder into blocks so that they could keep it. But it wasn't sweet like modern chocolate bars.

25 ## Health food

Today people like chilli chocolate, just like the Aztecs, and it is a very fashionable flavour. Doctors say that pure chocolate is good for us, because it contains important vitamins, but
30 only a little at a time! Too much sweetened chocolate can rot teeth and be fattening.

### Glossary

**cacao** a tropical tree

**Maya** ancient Indian civilisation from Central America from about 1000 CE

**CE** Common Era

**Aztec** civilisation that was dominant in Mexico before the Spanish Conquest of the sixteenth century

**jade** hard, green stone

**manufacture** make on a large scale using machinery

Pods from a cacao tree

# Comprehension

**A** **Write short answers to these questions.**

1 Who were the first people to discover cacao?

2 What did the Aztec people use cacao beans for?

**B** **With a partner, decide whether the statements below are true or false. Use the text to explain your answers.**

1 The pods from one cacao tree produce 20 grams of chocolate powder.

2 Chocolatl was a drink made with sugar.

3 Pure chocolate is unhealthy.

**C** **What about you?**

1 In small groups, talk about what foods you and your family eat on a special occasion such as a birthday. Suggest a reason why this food is eaten on your family's special occasion.

2 Think about a festival in your country and the food eaten during that time.

3 Describe a festival to a partner. Include how long it lasts, the time of year and the type of food you eat.

- Skim read the report to find specific details
- Identify the main ideas in the text
- Explain your ideas clearly to a partner

A molinillo is used to whisk chocolate.

A molinillo from Mexico

**Stretch zone**

- Do you know the history of your festival foods?
- When were they first eaten and how were they prepared?
- Did they come from your country or a different country?

**?**

**How much chocolate do you eat? Do you think we eat too many sweet things nowadays? What sort of diet is best for our health and wellbeing?**

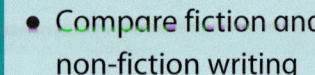

# Language for information texts

**A** Carefully read the two short paragraphs below. Think about the differences between the texts.

A cacao tree produces between 20 and 30 pods a year. Pods from one tree would make 450 grams of chocolate powder, about the same weight as a small bag of sugar. There are about 20 to 40 beans in each pod. (*The Origins of Chocolate* – an information, non-fiction text)

Charlie grabbed it and quickly tore off the wrapper and took an enormous bite… He was quite out of breath, but he felt marvellously, extraordinarily, happy. (*Charlie and the Chocolate Factory* – a fantasy narrative fiction text)

**B** Compare the types of words and features used in the fiction and non-fiction extracts (pages 16-17 and page 36). Copy and complete the table below by finding examples in the texts.

| Types of word and features | *The Origins of Chocolate* (page 36) | *Charlie and the Chocolate Factory* (pages 16–17) |
|---|---|---|
| Personal pronouns | it | he |
| Characters' names | | |
| Adjectives | | |
| Adverbs | | |
| Numbers | | |
| Subheadings | | |
| Direct speech | | |

**Language tip**
- Non-fiction writers often want to explain a process or a historical event.
- They use shorter sentences and include more facts, such as numbers and dates.

**C** Discuss these questions with a partner.

1 What is the purpose of the information text *The Origins of Chocolate*? What is the writer's reason for writing?

2 What is the purpose of the fantasy fiction text *Charlie and the Chocolate Factory*? How does the writer want to make the reader feel?

**Stretch zone**

Read a different non-fiction text and compare all the features to *The Origins of Chocolate*.

# Travelling vocabulary

> - Use a dictionary or thesaurus to look up new words
> - Work out the meaning of new words by looking at the context

**A** Copy the sentences below, filling in the correct word from the list.

> geysers    sea bridge    haka    chilli

1 The _____ is a traditional dance in New Zealand.

2 In Iceland, _____ can reach a temperature of nearly 100 degrees Celsius.

3 Two popular foods that originated in Mexico are _____ and chocolate.

4 The world's longest _____ is in China.

**B** Copy the travel words below. Write a definition of what each word means. Use a dictionary or a thesaurus to help you.

1 destination

2 excursion

3 currency

4 itinerary

5 reservation

**C** As a class, gather together interesting facts about different places in the world.

# The golden ticket to outer space

Do you want to buy a ticket to become an astronaut? Seven hundred people have already booked their **trip**. The first test flights have already taken place from a spaceport in the United States. Tickets cost as much as $250,000.

## A new kind of space ship

5   Richard Branson, a British airline owner and adventurer, has started a company called Virgin Galactic. They have built the spacecraft like the one you can see in the photo on page 41. The **mothership**, *WhiteKnightTwo*, has two compartments for crew, which look like two aeroplanes with a long **wingspan** in the middle. *SpaceShipTwo*
10  is **suspended** from the middle of the wing.

## How to become an astronaut

There will be two pilots and six passengers on *SpaceShipTwo*. *WhiteKnightTwo* will carry the spaceship up to 15.5 kilometres above the Earth, release it and go back to land. The spaceship's rocket will then **propel** it into space at up to 4,000 kilometres per hour. The
15  passengers become astronauts at 100 kilometres above the Earth. *SpaceShipTwo* will 'feather', or fold up, its wings. It will then fly higher to 110 kilometres and passengers will experience **weightlessness** for five minutes. They will be able to see the Earth's curve because they are so far away. Then the spaceship will re-enter the Earth's
20  atmosphere. At 21.5 kilometres the wings will de-feather (open out) so that it can glide down to the spaceport and land like a plane.

**Glossary**

**mothership** plane from which other spaceships are launched

**wingspan** length of the wings

**suspended** hung

**propel** push

**weightlessness** freedom from Earth's gravity so that you float

**gravity** force that pulls things down to the Earth

The passenger cabin of *SpaceShipTwo*. If you were not strapped in you would float around. This is because you would be weightless as there is no **gravity** far from the Earth.

# Comprehension

- Find the answers to questions
- Share ideas and explain your opinions
- Use information to make predictions

**A** Write your answers to the questions below. Use complete sentences.

1 How high does the mothership take *SpaceShipTwo* before it is launched?

2 When do the passengers become astronauts?

3 What makes passengers weightless?

4 What happens to *SpaceShipTwo's* wings during the flight?

5 How does gravity stop us from being weightless?

**B** 1 Explain in your own words whether you think it is a good or a bad idea to take tourist trips into space. Use the text to help you.

2 With a partner, prepare a short report on either the dangers of space travel for tourists or the benefits of it. Present this to the class.

**C** 1 What do you think spacecraft might be used for in 30 to 50 years? Discuss your ideas with a partner.

2 If there are people flying all round the world in spacecraft in the future, what ideas do you have to keep people safe?

3 Write a report containing your ideas for the future use and safety of space travel. Include a summary and paragraphs with subheadings. Illustrate your report.

**Stretch zone**

How does weightlessness and the lack of gravity make it difficult to live in a spaceship?

Make a list of the problems.

The mothership carrying *SpaceShipTwo* into the air to be launched.

- Read a non-chronological report

## Model writing

# London

London, the capital city of the United Kingdom, is set on the River Thames in the southeast of England.

### Facts

London is one of the biggest cities in Europe and has a population of almost 9 million people, which is more than 12 per cent of the United Kingdom's overall population. It was the first city in the world to have an underground railway.

### Historical Sites

There are many historical sites worth visiting in London. The Houses of Parliament is the seat of government and sits beside the River Thames. Nearby is the famous Big Ben. 'Big Ben' is the name of the largest bell inside the clock tower, not the tower itself. Westminster Abbey, where many British kings and queens were crowned, is another well-known tourist attraction. On the other side of the river is the London Eye, an **observation wheel** which gives impressive views of the city. For some people the most famous historical site in London is Buckingham Palace, the London home of Queen Elizabeth II.

### Culture

There are over 100 theatres in London showing a wide variety of musicals and plays. The most famous is probably The Globe which was built in the 1990s. The playwright William Shakespeare's plays were performed in the **original** theatre in the 1600s. London has a number of excellent museums, such as the Science Museum and Natural History Museum.

### Shopping

London has many places to shop, from world-famous shops on Oxford Street to the fashion stores of Carnaby Street, not forgetting two of the most famous shops in the world: Harrods department store and Hamleys toy shop.

London is visited by millions of tourists each year. There is certainly something for everyone and it is not necessary to spend a lot of money as many **attractions** are free.

- Research, plan and write a non-chronological report

# Report writing

The description of London is an example of a non-chronological report. These reports give factual information about a particular topic and are **not** written in time order.

## Features of non-chronological reports include

- Present tense
- Formal style
- Third person
- Subject-specific vocabulary
- Factual description
- Subheadings to group information

**Choose a capital city that you would like to visit.**

1   Do some research and make notes about the city, for example what you would like to see, the history of the city, the transport, food and language spoken.

2   Divide the information into headings and list specific vocabulary you will use under each heading.

3   Plan your non-chronological report using a writing frame like the one below.

4   Write up the report for your chosen city. Make sure you include the features of non-chronological reports.

| | |
|---|---|
| **Title** | |
| **Introduction** | |
| **First paragraph** | |
| **Second paragraph** | |
| **Third paragraph etc.** | |
| **Final summary** | |

On the map below, try to work out where each of the cities you've written about would be placed.

North America

Europe

Asia

Atlantic Ocean

Pacaific Ocean

Pacific Ocean

Africa

Indian Ocean

South America

Oceania

> "A robot may not injure a human being or allow a human being to come to harm."
>
> Isaac Asimov

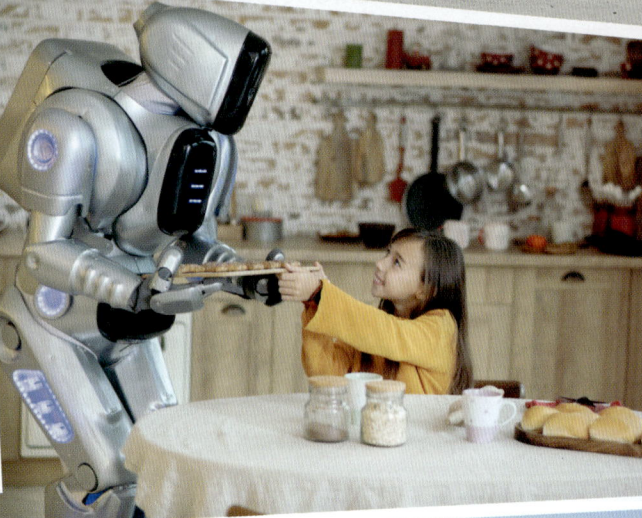

## Talk time

Modern robots are very clever. As technology develops, robots can look and act more like humans.

1 Look at the robots on this page. What are they doing?

2 What do you think robots might be able to do in the future?

## 3A Fiction Speaking, listening and vocabulary

- Share ideas and explain your opinions
- Use a dictionary to check meanings

**A** Match the words with their definitions below. Check your answers in a dictionary.

> robot   technology   science fiction
> bomb disposal   intelligence

**1** the study of science and machinery to make things work for people

**2** a machine that moves like a human or does the work of a human

**3** stopping a bomb from exploding

**4** the ability to think and learn

**5** stories set in the future

**Language tip**
Words that end with **-logy** often mean the study of something. For example, **biology** means the study of living things.

**B** Talk to a partner about the differences between robots and humans.

**1** Make a list of things that a robot might be able to do, but a human could not.

**2** Make a list of some human qualities that robots do not have.

**C** Imagine you are living in the future. Describe how robots might help you at home and at school.

Might robots become too powerful? Some people worry that robots will become too clever, learn to think for themselves and start to control humans. Many science fiction stories have been written about this. Do you think that robots might become more powerful than humans? Explain the reasons for your answer.

## Petey the robot

This is part of a story about a robot, Petey, who lives with Sam and Sophie. Petey's job is to help around the house but recently he has been behaving oddly. He is trying to sneeze and cough. He is also trying to write poetry and draw pictures. Sophie is very puzzled about this non-robotic behaviour.

My brain was working **overtime** – how could this be happening? There had to be a reason.

Petey, do you mind if I open up your front panel and take a look inside?

Of course he didn't mind. I whipped my trusty electro-screwdriver from my back pocket and opened the panel at the front of his chest.

Sam and I peered in at the **jumble** of frayed wires in there.

Bit of a mess isn't it?

Must be ages since anyone looked in here.

5    I poked around a bit further.

Hold on – what's this?

I pulled out a thick **knot** of wires to look at it more closely. But then I saw it was more than just wires. There was something in the middle of it – something alive!

It was a tiny brown creature with a little pink nose and a long tail. It let
10  out a tiny squeak.

'What is it?" I yelped.

From *Petey* by Paul Shipton

# Comprehension

Find information in the story

Use clues in the story to answer questions

Recognise direct speech and how it is presented

**A** Talk to a partner about these questions.

1 Why did Sophie want to open Petey's front panel?

2 What do you think the children found in the middle of the wires? Explain your thinking.

**B** Write answers to these questions.

1 What does the 'jumble of frayed wires' tell us about Petey?

2 What do we learn about the relationship between Sophie and Petey?

3 Describe the two ways that the writer presents direct speech.

**C** Talk to a partner about these questions.

1 How do you think the children's discovery might explain the change in Petey's behaviour?

2 Why do you think the writer presents direct speech in two ways?

3 The writer uses narrative, as well as speech, to tell the story. What information does the narrative give us?

**Language tip**
Remember that a **narrative** describes what happens.

● Listen to and read a list poem

## List poem

This poem shows how we use words all the time in different ways and for different reasons.

### Words Are Ours

In the beginning was the word
and the word is ours:
the names of places,
*the names of flowers,*
5  the names of names,
words are ours.
**Page-turners**
for **early-learners**
*How to boil an egg*
10  or mend a leg
Words are ours
Wall-charts
Love hearts
*Sports reports*
15  Short **retorts**
*Jam-jar labels*
Timetables
Words are ours
Following the instructions
20  for furniture constructions
Ancient **mythologies**
Online **anthologies**
Who she wrote for
Who to vote for
25  Joke collections
Results of **elections**
Words are ours
The tale's got you gripped

Have you learned your script?
30  The method of an Experiment
Ingredients for merriment
W8n 4ur txt
Re: whts nxt
Print media
35  Wikipedia
Words are ours
Sub-titles on TV
Details on your cv
Book of great speeches
40  *Guide to the best beaches*
Looking for chapters
on **velociraptors**
Words are ours
The mystery of history
45  The history of mystery
The views of news
The news of views
*Words to explain*
*the words for pain.*
50  doing geography
Autobiography
What to do in pay-phones
*Goodbyes on gravestones*
Words are ours.

Michael Rosen

### Glossary

**page-turners** exciting books

**early-learners** young people learning

**retorts** angry replies

**mythologies** collections of myths

**anthologies** collections of poems or stories

**elections** voting for people

**velociraptors** small, meat-eating dinosaurs

- Find details in the poem to answer questions
- Make notes comparing poems

## Comprehension

**A** Find a line in italics from the poem to match each description below. Write down both of them. The first one has been done for you.

1 The 400 metres race was won by Maria Flores.
   *Sports reports*

2 The beach is cleaned every morning.

3 IN LOVING MEMORY OF HENRY DAVIS

4 Strawberry Jam, Hilltop Farm

5 A daffodil is a spring flower.

6 Pain: the feeling in your body when you are hurt

7 Place the egg in a pan of boiling water.

**B** Write a short paragraph on each question.

1 What do you think a book called 'The mystery of history' (line 44) would be about?

2 In what way would a book called 'The history of mystery' (line 45) be different?

**C** Look back at 'Finding a friend' on page 50. In what ways is it similar to 'Words Are Ours' and in what ways are the two poems different?

**Stretch zone**

Find some other poems that Michael Rosen has written in the form of a list. Make notes on the style and topics of these. Do they rhyme? Are they funny? Share your ideas with a partner and see if they have the same ideas as you.

- Read a science fiction story

## Petey the robot (continued)

Read the extract below, which continues the story of Petey. Sam and Sophie's parents want to get Petey 'fixed', but Sam and Sophie have grown fond of the new Petey. They want to keep him just as he is.

### Glossary

**jet-pack** rocket belt or backpack that can make you fly

We raced into the kitchen.

'A Corrections Squad is on its way,' I said. 'They're going to fix you!'

How long have we got?

Their adverts always say that they answer every call within 10 minutes!

He looked terrified. He would do anything to get away from the Corrections Squad.

But... but... what can we do? We can't out-run a Corrections Squad jet-van.

5     'Yes we can,' said a voice from the doorway. It was Sam.

He had strapped his jet-soccer **jet-pack** onto his back. In his hands he held out two of Dad's old jet-packs.

We can get away if we use these!

10     He was grinning, but I knew him too well. I could see the fear in his eyes.

Sam, are you sure?

Sam knew what I meant. He was bad enough with a jet-pack in the jet-soccer playing zone. Flying through the crowded airways of the city was even more difficult… and dangerous.

But Sam gave a determined nod.

From *Petey* by Paul Shipton

- Plan and make notes for writing
- Write a playscript
- Perform a playscript

# Guided writing

**1** Talk with your partner about how you could rewrite this extract as a playscript. Think about:

- Which main characters speak
- What the stage directions will describe.

**2** Complete the playscript started below.

*(Sam and Sophie raced into the kitchen)*

**SOPHIE** A Corrections Squad is on its way. They're going to fix you!

## Your writing

**3** Talk to a partner about what might happen next in the story.

Think about:

- Whether Sophie and Petey agree with Sam's idea.
- What happens when the Corrections Squad arrives.
- Whether the jet-packs work.
- Whether there is an exciting chase.
- What happens in the end.

**4** Choose some of the ideas you talked about. Make brief notes to plan what happens.

**5** Use your notes to write your playscript in full.

## Performance

**6** In small groups, read out your playscript and plan a performance.

Think about:

- your movements and expressions
- your voice – it should be clear and loud so the audience can hear
- how to make the performance exciting and/or funny.

# Revise and check (1)

## Vocabulary

**1** Complete the sentences with adverbs made from the words below.

> excited   kind   anxious   furious

**a** The parents were worried and waited _____ for their children to arrive.

**b** It was his birthday and he ran _____ towards the letterbox.

**c** He slammed the door _____ and ran out into the yard.

**d** She felt sorry for the child and spoke to her _____.

**2** Choose a more interesting word than 'said' in these sentences. Use words from the list below.

> shouted   asked   screamed   explained

**a** "Is there a storm coming?" the boy said.

**b** "There are always storms here in October," said the Captain.

**c** "Hey! Be careful!" he said to the boy.

**d** "Oh no!" said the boy, as the wave hit.

**3** Answer these questions on metaphor:

**a** Would the metaphor 'an orchestra of drums and trumpets' best describe a storm or a cacao tree?

**b** Give reasons for your answer to 3a.

**c** Write a metaphor to describe your favourite fruit.

## Punctuation

**1** Add the correct punctuation to this passage:

Sam and Sophie noticed that Petey was behaving oddly.
He's been writing poems said Sam.
Are they any good asked Sophie.
No sighed Sam. But I also saw him singing dancing and trying to do some yoga!

# Grammar

**1** Copy and complete the table with the missing adjectives
and adverbs.

| Adjective | Adverb |
|---|---|
| cheerful | _____ |
| _____ | quickly |
| polite | _____ |
| _____ | happily |
| silent | _____ |

**2** Rewrite the sentences below. Use words from the table above
to fill in the gaps.

They welcomed the new girl c_____. She was s_____
at first but then answered their questions p_____. She
didn't make friends q_____ but by the end of the week she
looked h_____.

# Spelling

**1** Choose the correct ending to complete these words.

> -or    -ar    -er

**a** lawy____        **c** govern____

**b** burgl____        **d** caterpill____

**2** Turn the words below into adjectives by writing
the words with the correct suffix.

> -al    -ful

**a** help        **d** nation

**b** tradition        **e** nature

**c** thought

**3** Rewrite this paragraph. Add the suffix **-ing**
to the root words in brackets.

They heard the waves (explode) and (hit)
the side of the ship. Thunder was (roar)
and (rumble) in the distance and there
was no sign of the storm (stop).

**"There have been great societies that did not use the wheel, but there have been no societies that did not tell stories."**
Ursula K. LeGuin

## Talk time

1 These pictures show traditional stories and how they are passed from one person to another. Talk about what you think is happening in each picture.

2 In groups, look at a tale or legend and then tell the class briefly what it is about. What is the moral or purpose behind the story?

- Summarise a tale or legend
- Recognise traditional story vocabulary
- Identify features of tales and legends

**A** Match the words with their definitions.

> fable   legend   loyalty   quest   trickster   values

*Example:* an ancient story which has been passed down through the ages = legend

an ancient story which has been passed down through the ages

a person who lies to cheat other people

the important things in life that people believe in and act upon

a special search involving a journey

faithfulness to a friend or a family member

a story which teaches a lesson about how people should behave

## Typical features of traditional tales and legends

**Characters:** talking animals or fantasy creatures, wizards, queens, kings, rich and poor, good and evil, wise and foolish

**Actions to show:** courage and determination, kindness, helpfulness, patience

**Settings:** a long journey, a long time ago, dangerous places, palaces, mountains, lakes

**Themes:** a gift or an object with special and unusual powers, a quest to find a person or an object, a reward or punishment

**Narrative structure:** repetition; a predictable plot including a problem, a crisis and a solution, with a happy ending.

Aesop is believed to be a storyteller from ancient Greece, but we don't know whether he really existed.

• Read a traditional tale

Tchang is on his way to visit the Great Wizard of the West. Tchang needs to ask the Wizard why he and his mother are so poor. On his journey, Tchang meets three others who also have questions for the Wizard.

**Glossary**

**jiffy** moment
**carved** carefully cut
**bellowed** shouted loudly

## Tchang and the Pearl Dragon

Tchang was about to run away, but the dragon called to him. "Don't be frightened! I'm quite harmless. Tell me why you want to cross my river."

Tchang explained that he needed to ask the Great Wizard of the
5 West some important questions.

When the Pearl Dragon heard the questions, it smiled. "You're a good lad, Tchang," it said. "Hop on my back and I'll have you across in a **jiffy**."

On the far side of the river, Tchang thanked the dragon.

10 "Think nothing of it!" the dragon replied cheerfully. "That's what I'm here for. Oh, by the way. While you're there, could you please ask the Wizard why I can't fly? Every dragon in China can fly – except me." Naturally, Tchang said yes. He set off again towards the West with the four questions going around and around in his head.

15 Forty-nine days later, he came to the golden palace of the Great Wizard of the West. The palace was **carved** out of a mountain. It took Tchang a whole day to climb the million steps up to the huge door. When he pulled on the bell rope, the mountain shook.

The great doors of the palace swung open. Tchang found himself
20 in a mighty hall. On a throne at the end of the hall sat the Great Wizard. "Well?" he **bellowed**. "What do you want, boy?"

Tchang tried to stop shaking. "I… I have four questions to ask you, sir!"

"HAH!" shouted the Wizard. "Then you may as well go home right
25 now! I will only answer THREE questions. If you ask me four, I won't answer any of them!"

Tchang thought his legs would fold underneath him. What could he do? There was his poor mother's question, then the old woman's question, then the old man's question, and then the Pearl Dragon's
30 question. He desperately wanted to know the answer to the first question, but he also knew he couldn't let his friends down. So he answered sadly, "Then I will only ask you three."

From *Dragon Tales* by Andy Blackford

# Comprehension

**A** Write the events below in the correct order. You may need to skim read the story again.

1. It took Tchang a day to climb up the million steps to the door of the Wizard's palace.

2. Tchang was afraid to ask the Wizard his questions.

3. The Pearl Dragon told Tchang to ask the Wizard why he couldn't fly.

4. Tchang hopped on the dragon's back in order to cross the river.

**B** With a partner, discuss the questions below, then write the answers.

1. How do Tchang's feelings change between these events below?

   **a** When Tchang thanks the dragon for giving him a ride

   **b** When he first speaks to the Wizard

   **c** When he realises he can only ask three questions

   Find evidence from the story to support your answers.

2. Find two different words that show the wizard's anger.

3. Find two features of traditional tales and legends that the writer has used in Tchang's story.

**C** 1. Why do you think the Wizard will only answer three questions and no more? Discuss your ideas with a partner.

2. Write the next part of this traditional story. Choose either **a** or **b** below as your starting point.

   **a** The dragon persuades Tchang to go back in to see the Wizard and try again.

   **OR**

   **b** Tchang travels home with only three answers and meets his questioning friends on the way.

- Skim the story for key events
- Find evidence to support answers
- Recognise features of traditional tales
- Write a new scene

**?**

Writers of traditional tales and legends often use a story to teach a lesson about behaviour. What do you think the lesson of this story might be? Why do you think writers use a story rather than just telling the reader how to behave?

## Pronouns

Pronouns are used to replace nouns so that we do not keep repeating the nouns. The writing below does not use any pronouns, so it is difficult to understand.

Jack asked Henry's mother if Jack could play with Henry and May. Henry's mother replied that Henry and May had just gone out with Ashok, Usha and Fatima, and that Henry, May, Ashok, Usha and Fatima had all gone to the park. Jack was very disappointed. Jack really wanted to play with Henry, May, Ashok, Usha and Fatima.

**A** Copy and complete the text below, using these pronouns.

| they | them | He | they | he | She |

Jack asked Henry's mother if _____ could play with Henry and May. _____ replied that _____ had just gone out with Ashok, Usha and Fatima, and that _____ had all gone to the park. Jack was very disappointed. _____ really wanted to play with _____ .

There are different types of pronouns.

| **Personal pronouns** | These replace a noun in a sentence. | *I, you, me, him, she, he, her, they, we, them, us, it* |
|---|---|---|
| **Possessive pronouns** | These replace a noun and also show ownership. | *theirs, mine, yours, his, hers, its, ours* |

**B** Choose three personal pronouns and three possessive pronouns. Write six sentences, using each pronoun correctly.

**C** With a partner, list the pronouns used in the story on page 60. What type of pronouns are they?

**Stretch zone**

The word 'himself' (line 19 of *Tchang and the Pearl Dragon*) is a reflexive pronoun. Write down other reflexive pronouns that you can think of.

- Understand how to use commas

# Commas

**Commas** can be used in different ways within a sentence.
- To separate a main clause from a subordinate clause
- To separate words and phrases.

**A** The examples below from *Tchang and the Pearl Dragon* show the different ways commas can be used. Copy the grid and write your own examples in each row. You could take some other examples from the story and make up others of your own.

| When to use a comma | Examples from *Tchang and the Pearl Dragon* |
|---|---|
| To separate a main clause from a subordinate clause | • When the Pearl Dragon heard the questions, it smiled. |
| Before 'but' | • Tchang was about to run away, but the dragon called to him. |
| After a prepositional phrase or an adverbial | • Forty-nine days later, he came to the golden palace of the Great Wizard of the West. |
| Before directly addressing someone | • "You're a good lad, Tchang." |
| To separate phrases in a list | • There was his poor mother's question, then the old woman's question, then the old man's question. |

**B** With a partner, look in a fiction book to find commas. Choose three different sentences to show different ways that the comma is used. Write out the sentences.

**C** Make up six sentences, each of which use commas in one of the ways listed in the table in activity A. Then remove the commas – or put them in the wrong place – and ask a partner to correct the sentences.

# Possessive apostrophes

Apostrophes can be used to show belonging. They are called **possessive apostrophes**.

*Examples:* the man's house, the girls' hats, the children's bags

**A** Write out the following in the possessive apostrophe form.

*Example:* the cat belonging to the girl = the girl's cat

1 the tail belonging to the horse

2 the fields belonging to the farmer

3 the rice bag belonging to the lady

4 the supermarket belonging to the town

**Language tip**
The owner is always the one with the apostrophe.

If the owner is plural and ends in the letter **s**, the apostrophe has to be placed after the **s**. This makes singular and plural owners look different for the reader.

*Examples:*
the boots belonging to the boy (singular) = the boy's boots
the boots belonging to the boys (plural) = the boys' boots

If the owner is plural and doesn't end in a letter **s**, the apostrophe has to be placed after the owner.

*Examples:*
the boots belonging to the children (plural) = the children's boots
the van belonging to the men (plural) = the men's van

**B** Write out the following in the plural possessive apostrophe form.

1 the cats belonging to the girls

2 the tails belonging to the horses

3 the fields belonging to the farmers

4 the rice bags belonging to the ladies

**C** Some plural words do not end with an s. These words just add 's to show possession. Use the words below to write four sentences using the possessive apostrophe.

children   men   women   sheep

# Contraction apostrophes

Apostrophes can also be used when two words are shortened and joined together or contracted. An apostrophe shows that one or more letters are missing. These are called **contraction apostrophes**.

*Examples:* it is = it's, you are = you're

In *Tchang and the Pearl Dragon*, there are some examples of apostrophes used where words have been contracted.

**A** 1 **Write these contractions out in their full form. The first one has been done for you.**

| | |
|---|---|
| don't | do not |
| I'm | |
| I'll | |
| that's | |
| you're | |
| can't | |
| couldn't | |

**Language tip**

For the shortened form:

it is = it's

**use apostrophe.**

For the possessive form:

its = belonging to it

**no apostrophe.**

2 **Which one of the three reasons below is correct?**

Contraction apostrophes are used in texts because:

**a** they make the text easier to read

**b** they show how people speak informally to one another

**c** they vary the language and make it more interesting.

**B** One contraction in the story on page 60 changes letters as well as taking out letters. With a partner, find this word. Write:
- one sentence using the contracted word with an apostrophe
- another sentence using both words written in full form.

# Gelert, the Prince's Hound

A stone **monument** stands in a field on the outskirts of a village in North Wales. It marks the grave of 'Gelert', the faithful hound of the prince, Llywelyn the Great.

**Glossary**

**monument** statue to remind people of a person or an event

**leashes** straps or cords for holding on to a dog

**spurred** urged forwards

**suspicion** uncertain feeling about someone or something

**fiend** an evil spirit

**scored** scratched

Long ago, there lived a great prince in Wales called Llywelyn. The thing he loved best in the whole world was to play with his young son. His second favourite thing was to ride out of his castle at sunrise, leading his pack of hounds, as the
5  huntsman sounded his horn and the deer bounded ahead over the frosty ground to escape.

One day, Llywelyn decided to hunt. He called his huntsmen, mounted his horse and looked over the hounds who were barking joyfully and straining at their **leashes**. He frowned. Gelert, the
10 leader of the pack and the Prince's favourite hound, wasn't there.

"Where's Gelert?" he demanded.

No one could answer. No one had seen the great dog since the day before.

"We'll have to go without him," said Llywelyn. He **spurred** his horse forward.

At the end of the day, the huntsmen trotted back to the castle proudly bearing
15 a pair of fine stags. As they approached the castle, Gelert came limping out.

Llywelyn leaped down from his horse and ran inside. A terrible **suspicion** made his heart pound with fear. Whose blood was smearing the dog's coat, and staining his knife-sharp claws?

"My son! Where's my son?" he shouted.

20 He raced to the room where his little son should have been lying peacefully sleeping in his cradle. There was no sign of the child. The cradle was turned upside down, the bed clothes were torn, and it was clear that a terrible struggle had taken place.

"You murdering **fiend**!" roared Llywelyn, and raised
25 his dagger.

Gelert looked up at him one last time, his eyes filled with grief and shock, and died.

Then Llywelyn heard a little cry. He lifted up the cradle, and there, quite unharmed, lay his son.
30 Beside him lay the body of a gigantic wolf. The creature's skin was **scored** by the marks of a hound's claws, and deep bites scarred its face.

- Share ideas and explain your opinions
- Understand and use synonyms
- Write a new ending

"Oh, my faithful Gelert, what have I done?" cried Llywelyn. "You saved my son's life, and I killed you for it."

35 He carried Gelert's body out of the castle, and buried it in a place where all who passed by could see it and learn the story of the faithful hound. A pile of stones was set over the place where Gelert lies, and the castle was renamed Beddgelert, which means the Grave of Gelert.

Adapted from a retelling by Elizabeth Laird

## Comprehension

**A** Read the statements about the story. Which two are correct? Write out the correct sentences, giving evidence from the story to support your answer.

1 Llywelyn thought there was something wrong even before he entered the castle.

2 The baby was screaming.

3 Gelert killed the wolf.

4 Llywelyn didn't want people to know what he had done.

**B** Rewrite the sentences below. Change the underlined word with a word from the list (a synonym).

> urged    belief    glared    placed

1 He <u>spurred</u> his horse forward, unwilling to delay the hunt.

2 Llywelyn <u>stared</u> down at him in dismay.

3 A terrible <u>suspicion</u> made his heart pound with fear.

4 A pile of stones was <u>set</u> over the place where Gelert lies.

**C** In groups, discuss Llywelyn's reaction. Could he have acted differently? Talk about an alternative ending to the story.

**Stretch zone**

Many cultures have similar tales, but different animals replace the dog and the wolf. With a partner, write another version of the tale using different animals.

In Ancient Greece, the Greeks are at war with the Trojans. The Trojans are trapped inside their walled city. Each day, Karis climbs the walls to view the battle so she can tell her mistress.

## The Wooden Horse

So here I am, up on the walls again. It's still early. The sun is just coming up. Slowly, the mists clear on the **plain**.

And I can't believe my eyes!

"There's a big wooden horse down there!" I cry out to my
5  friendly **sentry**.

Then we both look beyond the horse.

"The Greeks have gone!" gasps the sentry.

It's true. The beach is completely empty. During the night the Greeks have packed their tents and slipped away in their ships.

10  Another sentry comes running up. He shakes his spear in the air in triumph. "The Greeks have given up! We've won the war!"

The good news spreads through Troy, as fast as flying arrows. "The Greeks have gone!" People shout it from the tops of our highest towers.

But why did they go? Everyone has their own explanation.

15  "It's because the gods have turned against them."

It's because their hero, **Achilles**, is dead."

Then the huge gates are flung open. Men, women and children pour out onto the plain...

Frantically, everyone sets to work. They put rollers under the horse and
20  tie ropes around its neck. Even the smallest child pulls their hardest. I join in too, tugging the rope.

Will it go through the city gates? People hold their breath. But it just fits.

"Ha ha," laughs someone. "So much for clever
25  **Odysseus**! He should have made it taller!"

People are cheering as it rocks through the gates.

**Glossary**

**plain** large area of flat land without trees

**sentry** soldier guarding something

**Achilles** Greek soldier, killed during the Trojan War

**Odysseus** the Greek warrior who thought up the idea of the Trojan Horse

70

- Talk about viewpoint
- Skim read the story
- Tell the story from another viewpoint

But what's that clanking sound? It seems to come from inside the horse.

I listen again. I can't hear it now.

30   "You must have imagined it, Karis," I tell myself.

Adapted from *Helen of Troy* by Susan Gates

# Comprehension

**A**   **Write these events from the extract in the order that they happened.**

1   The wooden horse just fits through the gates.

2   People from the city pour through the gates.

3   Karis hears a noise from inside the wooden horse.

4   The sun is just appearing.

5   The plain is empty, apart from a wooden horse.

**B**   **With a partner, talk about the questions below. Then write your answers.**

1   Who is telling the story? Why do you think the writer chose to tell the story from her viewpoint? (Think about the style of the language.)

2   Why has the writer written about a past event in the present tense? (Think about how this makes you feel involved in the story.)

3   Find some short sentences in the extract. Why does the writer use them? What impact do they have?

**C**   **Imagine you are EITHER one of the people in the crowd OR one of the soldiers in the wooden horse. Write this extract of the story from their point of view.**

**Stretch zone**

Do you think the Trojans were foolish to bring the horse into their city? What do you think the Trojans should have done?

Anansi the spider is a **trickster** in many African and Caribbean folk tales. He can change his shape to become a different character. In this story, Anansi is pretending to be a girl who is working for an Old Woman. The Old Woman refuses to pay for the work unless the girl (Anansi) can guess her name.

## How Crab Got a Hard Back

"Very well, girl," said Crab. "I promised to help you and I will." Crab whispered the name in Anansi's ear.

Anansi never even waited to say thanks. He ran up the bank of the stream without stopping to pick up the shoes when
5　they fell off. He ran to the Old Woman's home so fast that he was out of breath when he got there. The witch-woman shrieked, "Girl, can you guess my name?"

"I am not sure, ma'am," replied Anansi.

"Guess," screamed the Old Woman. "Guess three times.
10　Guess my name and you get the gold. Guess wrong and off you go."

"Your name is Mother Jane," cried Anansi.

"Wrong, wrong, first time wrong."

Anansi said slowly, "Your name is Mother **Jonkanoo**."

15　"Wrong, wrong, second time wrong. Guess again, then get along," cried the old witch-woman, and now her voice was like the crackling of fire in dry bush. She held her purse tight, for she was sure she would not have to pay out any money.

20　"Your name is Mother Cantinny," cried Anansi. "Mother Cantinny, Mother Cantinny." Anansi shouted the name aloud so that Parrot heard it and Kisander the cat also. The Old Woman fell to the ground as if she were dead. Then she got up, and gave Anansi half the clothes in the
25　**closet**, half the food in the cupboard, half the gold in the long, red purse. As he went off through the gate, Anansi laughed at her, "Anansi guessed your name, Old Woman, old Mother Cantinny!"

### Glossary

**trickster** someone who plays tricks on other people

**Jonkanoo** a dancing procession

**closet** wardrobe

## 4M Fiction Reading and comprehension

- Use evidence from the story to answer questions
- Explain why the writer used certain language
- Share ideas and discuss opinions

30 Mother Cantinny was very angry. "Anansi must have worked a trick on one of my children," she said to herself. She called them together, Duck, Goat, Peacock, and Crab, and stood them in a line.

She looked into the face of each one as she asked, "Who said Cantinny?"

35 She stared at Goat, and Goat stared back at her.

She stared at Duck, and Duck stared back at her.

She stared at Peacock, and Peacock stared back at her.

She stared at Crab, and Crab held his face down, looking at the ground.

40 "It's you, it's you," she cried. She threw the magic **calabash** at him. Crab turned and ran, but the calabash fell on his back, and the tears of all the girls **held it fast**. There it is. That is how Crab got his hard back. Anansi made it happen.

Adapted from *Tales From the West Indies* retold by Philip Sherlock

### Glossary

**calabash** fruit with a hard shell that comes from a tropical American tree

**held it fast** kept something in the same position

## Comprehension

**A** **Write answers to these questions.**

1 Sum up the story in four sentences.

2 Did the Old Woman expect Anansi to know her name? Write a sentence from the story that supports your answer.

3 How did the Old Woman find out that it was Crab who told Anansi her name?

**B** **Write answers to these questions.**

1 Why do you think Anansi pretended to make three guesses, even though he knew the correct name?

2 The verb 'stared' is used seven times in lines 35 to 38. Why do you think the writer chose to repeat this word? How many synonyms can you think of for 'stared'?

**C** **Would you be friends with Anansi? Explain your answer to a partner.**

 **Stretch zone**

Retell another Anansi story. If you don't know one, research them on the Internet. Choose one story to retell in your own words.

# Writing a traditional tale

## Model writing

- Read and discuss the structure of a story
- Use a model text to help plan and write a story

1 Read the traditional tale below. Look at the comments (in blue) which explain how the writer has structured the story. Notice how the story is introduced, the plot develops to a climax, then the problem is resolved.

### Grandmother Spider: A *Cherokee* Tale

In the beginning there was only blackness, and nobody could see anything. People said: "What this world needs is light."

> The story begins. The scene is set and the problem introduced.

Fox said some people on the other side of the world had plenty of light, but they were too greedy to share it. Possum said he would steal a little of it. "I have a bushy tail," he said. "I can hide the light inside all that fur."

> Characters are introduced. Dialogue moves the plot along.

Possum set out for the other side of the world. There he found the sun hanging in a tree and lighting everything up.

> The action moves forward in an imaginary world.

Possum sneaked over to the sun, picked out a tiny piece of light, and stuffed it into his tail. But the light was hot and burned all the fur off. Ever since, Possum's tail has been bald.

> The problem gets more complicated. Notice the strong verbs: 'sneaked' and 'stuffed'.

"I'll try," said Buzzard. "I'll put it on my head." He flew off and, diving straight into the sun, seized the light with his claws and put it on his head. It burned his head feathers off. And ever since that time, Buzzard's head has remained bald.

> The problem is repeated.

Grandmother Spider said, "Let me try!" First she made a clay pot. Next she spun a web reaching to the other side of the world. She was so small that nobody noticed her coming.

> The adverbs 'first' and 'next' help to move the story along.

Quickly, Grandmother Spider snatched up the sun, put it in the pot and scrambled back home along her web. Now her side of the world had light, and everyone rejoiced.

> Using lots of verbs close together gives the feeling of speed and action.

Grandmother Spider brought not only the sun to the Cherokee, but fire as well. And, she taught the Cherokee people the art of pottery making.

> The problem is resolved.

## Guided writing

**2**  Use the story structure shown in blue on page 74 to help you plan your own story. The questions below will also help you to plan your ideas.

- What is the main idea of your story?
- Where does it take place? What is the setting?
- Who are the main characters? What do they look like and how do they react to each other?
- The plot: what is going to happen? Think of a problem that needs to be resolved. How will this happen?
- What is the message of your story?
- Language techniques: think about using repetition, adverbs and strong verbs to move your story along.

**3**  Now write your story in full, following the structure you have planned.

**Learning tip**
**Swap** your planning notes with a partner. Suggest ways to improve each other's ideas.

"Oh, I get by with a little help from my friends"
John Lennon

## Talk time

1 What do you think this picture is about?

2 What different things can you see?

3 What would be in this picture if it was about you?

- Create a thought map
- Talk about similarities and differences
- Deliver and listen to a talk

# What makes you the person you are?

**A** Create a thought map of the things, activities and people that are most important to you. Look at the example below to give you some ideas.

- My parents and my grandparents
- Drama club
- Eating *goreng pisang* (banana fritters) at festival time
- My cousins in Kuala Lumpur
- My friends Laura, Nellie and Jake
- Playing basketball for my team
- Listening to music and buying new clothes
- Playing guitar
- My pet cat Fluffy

**B** **1** Compare your thought map with a partner's. What things are different? What are the same?

**2** What other things make up your **identity**? Look at the list below and decide which three are the most important.

> name    family    **personality**    food
> languages spoken    **nationality**
> home town or city    **culture**    hair and eye colour

**C** Every person is different. Like your fingerprint, no one else is exactly the same as you.

Plan a short talk to present to a small group in your class. You should include:

- a description of the items in your thought map
- an explanation of your choices about the three most important things that make up your identity.

**Glossary**

**identity** who somebody is

**personality** your nature and character

**nationality** the nation someone belongs to (as written on their passport)

**culture** all the traditions and customs of a group of people

# Home country, what's that?

In his interview, Hunter Emigh explains how he prepared for a presentation at his international school in Beijing.

### Hunter, where do you think of as 'home'?

It's not easy to give an answer to this question. I remember when I was in third grade our teacher asked us to do a research project on our 'home' country and give a presentation. I felt confused. I was born in
5  Texas, USA, but lived in Beijing, China. I liked my school in China and my friends. It felt like home.

### Where does your family come from?

My great grandmother was born in Germany, but lives in the USA. My great grandfather was born in Ireland, but lived in France. When I
10  hear the phrase 'home country' I think, what is that? My family come from all over the world.

Nearly all my grandparents had relatives in Germany. I spoke to my grandparents about their childhoods.

### What did you learn from your grandparents?

15  I learned about children growing up in Germany: how their language was different and how their school holidays were different. Even the **geography** of their land was different. I learned about German customs like the 'Schultuete', that's a special gift of sweets and school supplies that parents give their child on their first day of school.

### Glossary

**geography** the shape, climate and people

20  ### What did you present for your research project?

When it was time for the presentation, my teacher asked me, "Which country are you from?" Even though I was not born there, never lived there, and don't have any living relatives there, I proudly answered, "Germany". Really, I consider myself a person of the world.

25  ### What advice would you give to a student moving to a new region or country?

There is an old American saying, "Home is where you hang your hat". It means that wherever you live you can make a 'home' and
30  enjoy the culture and people that live there – no matter what your passport says. You don't have to forget or leave behind your family history, it's always a part of you wherever you live.

Adapted from *Slurping Soup and Other Confusions:* www.slurpingsoup.com

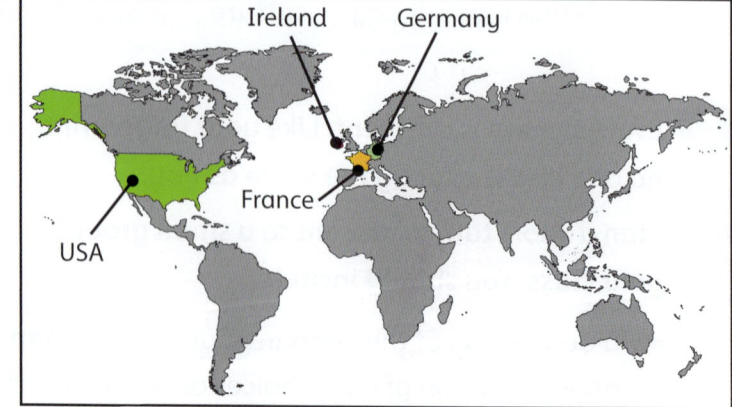

# Comprehension

**A** Write answers to these questions. Include evidence from the interview on page 78 to support your answers.

1 Which one fact about Hunter is true?

   **a** Hunter was born in the USA.

   **b** Hunter doesn't like his school in China.

   **c** Hunter's grandparents taught him about Chinese customs.

2 Which one statement best describes the extract?

   **a** It only contains facts.

   **b** It has only opinions.

   **c** It has both facts and opinions.

**B** Write answers to these questions using your own words.

1 Why does Hunter find it difficult to name his 'home country'?

2 Why was Hunter proud to choose Germany?

3 Give a short summary of the key points in each of Hunter's answers.

4 Write two more questions to ask Hunter that would help the reader understand more about his life.

**C** What about you?

1 With a partner, plan and write an interview about your life at school and where you consider 'home'. Look at the questions in the extract for ideas.

2 Present your interview to a small group in your class as a role-play.

**?**

"Children should learn about other countries and cultures to help them grow up to be a 'person of the world.'" Explain why you agree or disagree with this opinion.

# More pronouns

**Pronouns** are used in place of nouns.
*Examples:* I, me, we, you, she, her, he, him, it, they, them

- Identify pronouns and know who they refer to
- Identify pronouns that show the viewpoint in a text

**A** Write answers to these questions.

1  The non-fiction extract *Home country, what's that?* uses lots of different pronouns. Identify five.

2  Why do you think many pronouns are used in the extract? Choose one answer.

   **a**  To make it more personal

   **b**  It is largely about people and identity

   **c**  To make the text easy to understand and follow.

**Language tip**
Pronouns can be singular or plural. *Examples:* **I** and **we**.

The types of pronouns a writer uses can show what point of view the text is being written from.

| Point of view | Examples |
|---|---|
| First person | I, we, me, us |
| Second person | you |
| Third person | he, she, it, they, her, him, them |

**B** Are the following sentences written in the first, second or third person? Use the table above to help you.

1  I am going home to change my clothes.

2  They are going the wrong way.

3  We spent lunch break playing football.

4  You take 2 kilograms of flour and add 10 litres of water.

**C** Rewrite the sentences below. Change the pronouns to show another viewpoint.

1  Today it is Monday and I must get ready for school!

2  They are all going to the cinema.

3  We like to fly the kite on windy days.

# Plurals

- Learn the rules for plurals ending -ies, -es and -ves.

When a word is changed from singular (just one) to **plural** (more than one) the spelling changes.

Most words add **s**.
*Examples:* toy/toy**s**, book/book**s**, table/table**s**

If the word has a vowel (a, e, i, o, u) before the y, you just add **s**.
*Example:* key/key**s**

If the word ends in a consonant + y, change the **y** to **ie** before adding **s**.
*Example:* berr**y**/berr**ies**

## Tricky Spellings

Learn the plural spellings for words ending with 'o':

| | |
|---|---|
| **potato** | **potatoes** |
| **avocado** | **avoca<u>dos</u>** |
| **mango** | **mangoes** |
| **tomato** | **tomatoes** |

**A** Write the following words as plurals using the rules above.

boy   house   day   fly   city   meal   baby

**B** **1** The words in the grid opposite add **es** when they become plural. Work out why these words do this.
(**Clue:** Say the words aloud, and listen to the endings.)

**2** Write out the rule so that it is easy for another classmate to understand.

| Singular | Plural |
|---|---|
| box | boxes |
| dish | dishes |
| kiss | kisses |
| lunch | lunches |
| watch | watches |

When words end in **f**, or **fe**, and the **e** is silent, the **f** or **fe** is changed to **ves** in **plurals**.
*Examples:* cal**f**/cal**ves**, wi**fe**/wi**ves**

**C** Work with a partner to list and correct the five spelling errors in the extract below.

Everyone collected things for the picnic in the forest: knifes, loaves, cakes – and even scarfs and gloves in case it got cold! When they arrived, they found the ground covered in leafs. Everyone was enjoying themselfs, eating delicious food, talking and laughing, when some thiefs suddenly jumped down from the trees.

# Mary Seacole – A biography

Mary Seacole

## Early life

Mary Seacole was born in 1805 in Kingston, Jamaica. She had a good education and became interested in medicine and nursing. Her mother was a **traditional healer**, who taught Mary how to treat diseases and injuries.

## Panama

Mary married in 1836 but her husband died in 1844. After his death, Mary refused many other offers of marriage. In 1851, Mary went to stay with her brother in Panama. While she was there, a **cholera** epidemic broke out. The disease spread quickly and killed many people. Mary became well-known for her kindness in helping the sick.

## Crimea

After the start of the Crimean War in 1853, Mary decided to travel to the Crimea. In 1855, she opened the British Hotel near Balaclava in the Crimea. British officers who were sick or injured could pay to stay at the British Hotel where they could **convalesce**. They were served good food and were well cared for. Mary also travelled to the **battle front**, taking food and medicines. She looked after wounded and dying soldiers on both sides.

## London

When Mary returned to London in 1856, she was **bankrupt** from debts run up by soldiers at the British Hotel. The newspapers started a charity to raise money for her. The charity was supported by some members of the royal family and a grateful British Army. In 1857 her autobiography, *Wonderful Adventures of Mrs Seacole in Many Lands*, became a bestseller. Mary Seacole died in London in 1881.

### Glossary

**traditional healer** someone who uses old ideas to cure illness

**cholera** a severe infectious disease

**convalesce** get well again

**battle front** place where soldiers fight

**bankrupt** not able to pay the money you owe

Crimean War

# Features of a biography

- Look at the features of a biography
- Find information in the text to answer questions

A biography can be as detailed and descriptive as fiction writing. The difference is that it must be based on facts about a person's life. Some of the features of biographies are listed below.

- Events are told in chronological order
- Written in the third person
- Uses adverbials of time to show the sequence of events
- Includes facts about a person's life

**A**  With a partner, find examples of the features listed above in the biography of Mary Seacole on page 82.

**B**  These events in Mary Seacole's life are in the wrong order. Check the dates in the biography, then write the events in chronological order.

Crimea

- Mary opens the the British Hotel in the Crimea.
- Mary Seacole is born.
- Mary dies in London.
- Mary goes back to London.
- Mary's book about her adventures becomes a bestseller.
- Mary's husband dies.
- Mary goes to Panama.

**C**  Write answers to these questions.

1  Which two of the following statements are true?

   **a**  Mary Seacole was born in Jamaica.

   **b**  Mary remarried in 1851.

   **c**  Her autobiography became a bestseller.

2  Explain why Mary was bankrupt at the end of the Crimean War.

3  How did people show that they were grateful to Mary for caring for the British soldiers?

**Stretch zone**

Find out more about Mary's return to London in 1856. Write a biographical text about this period of her life. Remember to use the features listed above.

# Direct speech and reported speech

- In **direct speech** the words which are spoken go inside speech marks.

  *Example:* "She's the best player we've got," Clarence said.

- In **reported speech** someone is reporting or telling what someone else has said. It doesn't need speech marks or use exactly the same words as the spoken ones.

  *Example:* Clarence **told** the interviewer **that** Saanvi was the best player they had.

**A** With a partner, discuss which of the sentences below are direct speech and which are reported speech.

1 Mary Seacole said she wanted to nurse injured soldiers.

2 Hunter declared, "I'm from Germany!"

3 "I enjoyed reading the biography!" he exclaimed.

4 Salvador whispered that he had forgotten his homework.

**B** Change the direct speech in the sentences below to reported speech. The first one has been done for you. Notice the change of pronoun and the change of tense.

1 "I can finish the painting today," he said.

   He said **that he could** finish the painting that day.

2 "I really like swimming!" she declared.

3 "Can I interview you?" asked the boy.

4 "I hope you all like your new school," said the teacher.

**C** Write out the dialogue below, but change the two sentences in blue to reported speech.

"Are you coming to watch the game?" asked Maria.

"No," replied Juliet.

"Why not?" Maria said.

"I would rather watch a film on TV," Juliet explained.

"Oh, that's a shame," replied Maria.

She's the best player we've got.

When writing **direct speech**, the reporting clause can come:

● at the **start** of the sentence
*Example:* **She announced**, "In the interview, you can tell me all about your family!"

● in the **middle** of the sentence
*Example:* "In the interview," **she announced**, "you can tell me all about your family!" (Note that there is no capital letter in 'you' as it is not the start of a new sentence.)

● at the **end** of the sentence
*Example:* "In the interview, you can tell me all about your family!" **she announced**.

**Language tip**
Full stops, question marks and exclamation marks are usually part of direct speech, so put them **inside** the speech marks.

**A** Work with a partner to rewrite the sentences below, moving the reporting clause to the position shown in blue.

1 He exclaimed, "I hope when you play for our team, you will score many goals!" **end**

2 The head teacher announced, "I am glad to say there has been an improvement in behaviour, but not from everyone." **middle**

3 "If you practise hard you will be able to compete in the Olympic games," the coach whispered. **start**

Commas separate the reporting clause from the direct speech.
*Example:* He asked**,** "Why aren't you coming with me?"
"I think," he said**,** "I might come with you."

**B** With a partner, discuss where you would put commas in the sentences below, then rewrite them correctly.

1 "I would like to go to the beach this weekend" he said.

2 "I think" she replied "it would be a good idea."

3 She whispered "Marcenia is very upset."

**C** Write three of your own sentences which use direct speech. Put the reporting clause in a different place in each sentence.

# Sailing Solo

Laura Dekker, the youngest sailor to **circumnavigate** the globe single-handedly, arrived at the Caribbean island of St Maarten on 21st January 2012. She survived weeks at sea with just a few **cockroaches**
5 for company – and did her homework too.

She said, "I became good friends with my boat. I learned a lot about myself."

Laura alone at sea on *Guppy*

## She was born to sail

Her Dutch parents were living on a yacht in a port in New
10 Zealand when Laura was born, and she was six when she first sailed **solo**. At eight, she decided her dream was to sail round the world and, aged just 13, Laura sailed solo from the Netherlands to England and back.

## Dangers and discomforts

15 On her round-the-world trip she took on six metre high waves and extreme weather – on one occasion, heading to the Cape of Good Hope in Africa, her storm jib (a sail used in storms) got **jammed**. She finally managed to take it down in the early hours of
20 the morning. Another of her sails ripped completely during the voyage. She slept on a damp bed and lived on rice and pasta, with cookies and pancakes an occasional treat. She **dodged** near **collisions** with cargo ships and worried about pirates. Not in the least
25 squeamish, she had to rescue live flying fish that had flung themselves into her cabin. She survived weeks at sea with no company – except for the rats and cockroaches that had stowed away in her cabin. On top of all that, she had to do schoolwork.

Adapted from *The Guardian* January 2012

## Glossary

**circumnavigate** to sail around something completely

**cockroaches** insects

**solo** alone

**jammed** stuck

**dodged** moved quickly to avoid

**collisions** crashes

# Comprehension

**A** Write answers to the questions below. Use evidence from the text to support your answers.

1  What age was Laura when she first sailed solo?

2  Describe what happened to Laura near the Cape of Good Hope.

3  What dangers did Laura face, apart from the sea?

4  Write a summary sentence for each paragraph in the article. Each sentence should include a key fact.

**B** Work with a partner to write answers to these questions.

1  If you were writing about Laura Dekker's life, where would you get information from?

2  Read through the extract again and write a different title for the article and suggest different subheadings.

**C** What about you?

1  What sports are popular in your country? What international success has your country had at them?

2  How would you try to persuade adults to let you do something new and difficult, such as sail a boat on your own?

- Find information to answer questions
- Understand the difference between facts and opinions
- Talk confidently and clearly about your ideas

**?**

If you sailed around the world solo, what do you think you would enjoy? What do you think would be difficult? Should there be a minimum age for young people to travel alone? Give reasons for your answers.

*The Optimist* is a small sailing boat for children up to the age of 15. Laura sailed hers solo when she was six. They are simple, safe, and have only one sail. Children sail them in competitions.

*Arradon - Golfe du Morbihan*

# Single-clause and multi-clause sentences

- Recognise multi-clause sentences
- Make information simpler by using shorter sentences and easier vocabulary

The article about Laura Dekker uses long, multi-clause sentences and some specialist vocabulary. It would be hard for young readers to understand.

 **A** Look at the article again and compare it to this simpler version.

Laura Dekker is a young sailor. A sailor is a person who sails on boats in the sea, but sometimes it can be on rivers. Laura is the youngest person in the world to sail around the world on her own. Her trip ended on an island. This island is called St Maarten. It is in the Caribbean – which is near America.

Florida (USA)

Atlantic Ocean

St. Maarten

CUBA

**With a partner, talk about the differences in:**
- sentence length
- vocabulary
- the amount of information given
- the explanation of new terms.

**B** Rewrite the sentences below. Make them shorter and simpler for younger readers.

- At eight, she decided her dream was to sail around the world and by sixteen she had accomplished her plan.

- On one occasion, she took on six metre high waves while enduring extreme weather conditions.

**C** Look at the words in the Glossary on page 86 and their definitions. Choose four more words from the article that you think younger readers may not understand. List those words and write simple definitions for younger readers.

# Commas in multi-clause sentences

- Identify extra information in a sentence
- Use pairs of commas to separate extra information

> **Commas** can be used to separate off extra information about a person.
>
> *Example:* Laura Dekker, the youngest person to circumnavigate the globe, arrived at the Caribbean island of St Maarten.

**A** Copy the sentences below. Insert two commas in each sentence so that the extra information is separated off.

1 Mrs Brownlea the new principal is very popular.

2 Dan filled with despair slumped to the ground.

3 Lucian 15 years old decided to circumnavigate the globe.

**B** Rewrite each pair of sentences below as one sentence. You will need to change some of the words, as well as including commas around extra information.

1 Fatima Khan is an Olympic team member. She achieved her personal best in the high jump competition.

2 Andreas is the fastest cyclist in the world. He has won another gold medal.

3 Ahmed is 10 years old. He lost his front tooth yesterday.

**C** Rewrite the sentences below, making them simpler by taking out the extra information.

1 You need to revise for your exams, which are taken at the end of the year, in order to get a good mark.

2 Laura Dekker, who started sailing solo when she was 6 years old, circumnavigated the globe single-handedly.

3 The doctor, who is 34 years old, will see you in five minutes.

**Language tip**
Remember, the information between the commas is extra, non-essential information. A sentence should still make sense if you remove the two commas and this extra information.

# Keeping a diary

Laura kept a diary every day when she sailed round the world. She might have written like this.

## Monday, 6 December

I'm in the harbour at Cape Town today. Dad helped me to buy all my food and water for the next part of the trip. We packed everything carefully so that it can't get wet. I'm excited about leaving tomorrow morning.

## Tuesday, 7 December

I didn't sleep well because I was so nervous. This morning the sea was calm. Lots of people came to wave goodbye and some boats sailed beside me for the first few kilometres. Then I was all alone again.

## Wednesday, 8 December

The wind is perfect and I'm sitting here writing this in the sun. Lots of dolphins came and played around the boat and kept me company. I'm getting used to being by myself again. I tried to do some schoolwork this afternoon but dolphin watching is more fun.

## Thursday, 9 December

It began to get really rough and the waves crashed and the boat rolled along. It's still very rough. But the strong wind is good as we are going the right way. I've been wearing my waterproof clothes and staying in the cabin for hours to keep dry. I saw the cockroaches again. They have become my friends and I don't mind them.

## Friday, 10 December

It wasn't quite so rough today and the flying fish kept jumping into the boat. I don't like it when they smash on the deck or fall into the cabin. They smell if I don't get rid of them quickly. I hope I get a message tonight. I've sailed 150 kilometres since Tuesday. I miss my dog Spot. It would be nice to have him here, but dogs can't come on a journey like this.

- Understand the purpose of diaries
- Identify the features of a diary
- Write a diary using a suitable structure

# Features of diary writing

A diary is a personal record of someone's thoughts, feelings, events and experiences.

Features of a diary include:

**Date** – Sets an event or an experience in time

**First person** – The writer is writing about themselves

**Past tense** – The writer writes about what has happened

**Informal language** – The writer may not be writing for a general audience; details may be personal

**Adverbials of time** – The writer uses these to connect events and thoughts together

## Comprehension

**A** Read the diary carefully. Then write answers to these questions.

1 What do you notice about most of the verbs in the diary?

2 What pronoun does Laura use when she is writing about herself?

3 Does she write as if she's talking to a teacher or as if she's talking to friends?

**B** 1 How does the writer structure the diary to make it easy to follow?

2 Copy and complete the table on the right. Find evidence of each feature in the diary entries on page 90.

| Diary features | Evidence |
| --- | --- |
| Chronological order | |
| Thoughts and emotions | |
| Opinion | |
| First person narrative | |

**C** Pretend that you are Laura. Choose somewhere on the map on page 90 to start your journey. Write your diary for seven days. You can make up anything you like. Use a writing frame like the one below.

## My Diary

| Day 1 | |
| --- | --- |
| Day 2 | |
| Day 3 | |
| Day 4 | |
| Day 5 | |
| Day 6 | |
| Day 7 | |

91

## Writing an autobiography

- Plan paragraphs using a writing frame
- Use first person pronouns
- Check a partner's work and give feedback

**1** Write about yourself. Use a frame like the one below to plan your work. Then write three full paragraphs, following your plan.

### This is me! I'm happiest when I'm...

swimming…

in the sea at…

feeding my…

at home in the garden…

playing football…

in the park…

playing ice hockey…

at the ice-rink in…

---

I feel like…

The most important people in my life are…

My most precious possession is….

The best thing about my life is…

The strangest thing about my life is…

Sometimes I worry about…

when I'm…

because…

when…

while…

except…

especially…

---

### I'd describe myself as a...

friendly…

noisy…

quiet…

gentle…

outgoing…

confident…

thoughtful…

nervous…

anxious…

easy-going…

jokey…

…kind of person.

**2**  Now write about an event in your past when you felt worried or nervous. It could be when you started a new school or went on a journey.

Choose your words carefully, with plenty of description, so that the reader can feel what it was like to be there. Use the questions and vocabulary in the table below to help you plan your work.

| Questions to help you | Words and phrases you can use |
|---|---|
| **Setting – paragraph 1:** | |
| How old were you? | The thing that worried me most happened when I was _____ years old. |
| Where were you? Describe the place. | I was in/at/beside _____. It was dark/quiet/cold _____. |
| What time/day/month/season was it? | I knew it was ___ o'clock because _____ . |
| **Characters – paragraph 2:** | |
| Who were you with? | At the time, I was with _____. |
| What were they doing? | He/She was _____. |
| What were you doing? | I was _____because_____ |
| **What happened? – paragraph 3:** | |
| What was the problem? | Just then, /A moment later, /To my surprise, /Suddenly, _____. |
| How did it get worse? | What was worse, _____ I heard/saw/smelt _____. |
| Why were you worried? | I felt as if _____. |

**3**  When you have finished your first draft, swap with a partner. Give each other feedback before writing your final draft.

"Poetry remembers it was an oral art before it was a written art."

Jorge Luis Borges

## Talk time

1 Which is your favourite picture on this page? Why?

2 Each picture illustrates a different poem or story. With a partner, describe each picture and discuss what you think the poem or story might be about.

# Narrative poems

**A** All narrative poems tell a story. There is a list of famous narrative poems below. With a partner, read the list and decide which picture (A to D) links to which poem in the list. Talk about the reasons for your choices.

1 Humpty Dumpty
2 The Pied Piper of Hamelin
3 Lord Neptune
4 Little Red Riding Hood and the Wolf

**B** Here is a list of features found in most narrative poems:

- they tell a story with a series of events
- they include characters
- the story takes place in a specific setting
- the poem uses patterns of language, such as rhyme and rhythm
- the poem is divided into verses or stanzas
- the poem is meant to be read aloud.

With a partner, find your own example of a narrative poem containing some of these features. Present your narrative poem to the rest of the class.

- Discuss the features of narrative poems
- Research a narrative poem
- Read a narrative poem aloud

**People told each other narrative poems a long time before most people could read or write. Why do you think these story poems were so popular and important to people?**

## Soft Landings

Space-man, space-man,
**Blasting** off the ground
With a wake of flame behind you
**Swifter** than passing sound.

5  Space-man, ace-man,
Shooting through the air,
Twice around the moon and back
Simply because it's there.

Space-man, place-man,
10 **Cruising** through the skies
To plant your flags on landscapes
Unknown to human eyes.

Space-man—race, man,
**Scorching** back to earth—
15 To home and friends and everything
That gives your **mission** worth.

Howard Sergeant

### Glossary

**blasting** launching of a spacecraft

**swifter** quicker

**cruising** travelling at a steady speed

**scorching** burning

**mission** an important job someone is sent to do

## Comprehension

**A** **Write answers to the questions below, using the poem to help you.**

1 Who is waiting for the space-man at the end of his mission?

2 Make a list of the 'space' vocabulary you can find in the poem. Add any other space words you can think of to your list.

3 Match each verse with a summary word from the list in blue. Add one more word to the list, to summarise one of the verses.

| Return | Flight | Launch |
| --- | --- | --- |

Verse 1 _____

Verse 2 _____

Verse 3 _____

Verse 4 _____

**B** **Write answers to the questions below, using the poem to help you.**

1 What phrases does the poet use to describe the space flight?

2 Which phrase in each verse shows the progress of his journey?

3 The first line of each verse is nearly the same. Why do you think the poet did this?

**C** **Discuss these questions with a partner.**

1 Do you like the poem? Explain why or why not.

2 Would you like to visit space? Explain your answer.

- Understand the message of the poem
- Know the meaning of space-themed vocabulary
- Discuss the poet's choice of words

**Stretch zone**

Find some other poems about space. Discuss or note down the differences you find between these poems and 'Soft Landings'.

# Personification

- Identify the human qualities given to objects in the poem
- Talk about the language used by the poet

**Personification** gives an object human qualities, such as feelings, speech and movement. It is often used by poets to create an interesting picture in our minds.

*Example:*

> The moon was but a chin of gold
> A night or two ago,
> And now she turns her perfect face
> Upon the world below.

Emily Dickinson

Obviously the moon doesn't really have a face, but people do, so the poet is using personification to create an interesting picture in our minds.

**A** Copy and complete the sentences below by adding one of the verbs from the list. The first one has been done for you.

> ~~whispered~~   told   spat   groaned

1 The snow **whispered** as it fell from the night sky.

2 The machine _____ out the chocolate bar.

3 The old bed _____ as the children leapt on to it.

4 The clock _____ me that it was time to leave.

**Stretch zone**

Find nursery rhymes and songs that use personification.

**B** Copy the text below and circle the examples of personification. The first one has been done for you.

The oak tree in my garden (is an old friend to me). When I climb onto his knee, he wraps his long arms around me and he keeps me warm when he takes off his coat in winter. We moan to each other, especially when the wind blows, and he reaches down when the raindrops weigh heavily on his arms.

**C** With a partner, discuss the poem by Emily Dickinson. What is the 'chin of gold'? What does she mean by 'her perfect face'? Why does this change happen 'a night or two' later?

# Similes and metaphors

**Similes** and **metaphors** compare things to other things in order to make description more interesting and to add detail. They are often used in poetry.

Similes compare two things using the words **like** or **as**.

Metaphors compare two things by saying one thing *is* another thing.

- Work out the meaning of similes and metaphors
- Identify similes and metaphors
- Write your own similes and metaphors

 **1** Which two things in each sentence below are being compared?

    **a** The space-man flies like a bird.

    **b** My two best friends are like two peas in a pod.

    **c** The spaceship is as quick as lightning when it's on its way to the moon.

**2** Which two things in each sentence below are being compared?

    **a** The moon is a dinner plate.

    **b** Life is a rollercoaster.

    **c** Luis is a night owl.

**B** With a partner, decide which of these are similes and which are metaphors. Talk about what you think each simile or metaphor actually means.

**1** His bedroom was a zoo.

**2** This party is as much fun as going to the dentist!

**3** The news was music to my ears.

**4** My sister was like a fish out of water.

**C** Write a four-line poem containing the following:

Line 1   A simile about the sky

Line 2   A metaphor about clouds

Line 3   A simile about the rain

Line 4   A metaphor about a stream

## The Tale of Custard the Dragon

Belinda lived in a little white house,
With a little black kitten and a little gray mouse,
And a little yellow dog and a little red wagon,
And a **realio**, **trulio**, little pet dragon.

5  Now the name of the little black kitten was Ink,
And the little gray mouse, her name was Blink,
And the little yellow dog was **sharp as Mustard**,
But the dragon was a coward, and she called him Custard.

Custard the dragon had big sharp teeth,
10  And spikes on top of him and scales underneath,
Mouth like a fireplace, chimney for a nose,
And realio, trulio daggers on his toes.

Belinda was as brave as a barrel-full of bears,
And Ink and Blink chased lions down the stairs,
15  Mustard was as brave as a tiger in a rage,
But Custard cried for a nice safe cage.

Belinda tickled him, she tickled him **unmerciful**,
Ink, Blink and Mustard, they rudely called him **Percival**,
They all sat laughing in the little red wagon
20  At the realio, trulio, cowardly dragon.

Ogden Nash

### Glossary

**realio trulio** really, truly
**sharp as mustard** clever, alert
**unmerciful** without pity
**Percival** an un-heroic legendary character (who actually does a very heroic deed in the end)

## Comprehension

- Discuss how the story is told in the poem
- Identify similes and metaphors
- Discuss the poet's choice of words

**A** Write answers to the questions below, using the poem to help you.

1 What animals lived in the house?

2 How did the others all treat Custard?

3 Describe how Custard looked in your own words.

**B** Write answers to the questions below.

1 Which word is repeated in the first two verses? What is the poet trying to do by using this word again and again?

2 Find an example in the third verse of:

   **a** a simile

   **b** a metaphor.

3 What do this simile and metaphor tell us about Custard?

4 What other similes can you find in the poem and what is the poet telling us about the other characters by using these?

5 What effect does the repetition of 'realio, trulio' in lines 4, 12 and 20 have on you? Why do you think these words were misspelt?

**C** Discuss these questions in a small group.

1 In your groups, finish reading the poem together on pages 158–160. Have your ideas about the story in the poem changed? What have you now found out about Custard's character?

2 Is this a funny poem or a serious one? Give reasons for your answer.

3 Think of a moral for this story.

# Alliteration and onomatopoeia

- Recognise examples of alliteration and onomatopoeia
- Understand the effect of alliteration and onomatopoeia

**Alliteration** is when the same sound is used at the start of a number of words in a sentence. It can be used to create an effect in a poem.

*Examples:* The grumpy old goat grazed on the green grass.

Betty bought a bit of butter.

**Onomatopoeia** also uses sound to create an effect. It imitates the sound of what is being described.

*Examples:* The boys munched and crunched their food.

The rocket whooshed high up in the air.

**A**  Write your answers to these questions.

1 Which of the following is an example of alliteration?

a The river is a snake weaving down the valley.

b The water was as cold as ice.

c The sun shone on the smooth surface of the sea.

2 Which of the following contains an example of onomatopoeia?

a I could hear the pitter patter of raindrops on the parched soil.

b The storm started at six o'clock sharp.

c The lion's roar was like thunder in my ears.

3 'Crash!', 'ping!' and 'squeak!' are examples of:

a alliteration          b similes

c onomatopoeia

4 'The cat crept carefully around the corner' is an example of:

a personification          b alliteration

c onomatopoeia

**B**  Write a sentence containing alliteration using the letter A. Choose five more letters in the alphabet and write sentences with alliteration for each letter.

**Stretch zone**

Find examples of alliteration and onomatopoeia in poems. Look in poetry books in the classroom and research poems on the Internet.

- Recognise subordinating clauses and conjunctions
- Understand how to change the order of clauses

# Subordinate clauses and conjunctions

Subordinate clauses don't make sense on their own but need a main clause as well. These two clauses are joined together by a **subordinating conjunction**.

*Example:* The old man likes to go for a walk when the sun is shining.

main clause        subordinating conjunction        subordinate clause

The subordinate clause can also go first in the sentence.

*Example:* When the sun is shining, the old man likes to go for a walk.

Notice that there is a comma after the subordinate clause when it comes first.

**A** Copy and complete the sentences below using a subordinating conjunction from the list. Only use each one once.

> before    when    since    even though

1 He kept laughing _____ she had stopped tickling him.
2 The birds ate all the food _____ they flew away.
3 I have read five books _____ I joined the library last weekend.
4 Raj ran to the door _____ the doorbell rang.

**B** Rewrite these sentences so that the subordinate clause comes first. Circle the subordinating conjunction. Don't forget to add a comma in the correct place.

1 Custard felt safe as long as he was in his cage.
2 The squirrel ran up a tree after the dog chased it.
3 The astronaut climbed down from the spaceship in order to plant a flag on the moon.
4 Selma will be late for school unless she gets out of bed right away.

**C** Write three sentences that include one of the following subordinating conjunctions. Use each conjunction only once.

> once    if    until

Jesus Bauzo is a Puerto Rican poet. He wrote this poem because he felt that many young people today don't respect the 'young people of yesterday', many of whom gave their lives for us.

- Listen to and read a narrative poem
- Describe a character's thoughts and feelings

## The Old Man

It was a beautiful morning.
The sun was shining in all its glory,
But also warmed with all his **ardor**.
The old man was walking through the beautiful **sidewalk**.
5   He walked alone and in silence.
He was **accompanied** only by his old cane,
And by his old round hat.
Always walking upright and facing forward.
Several young men came running
10  by his side and they **mocked** him…
The old man continued walking in silence.
Minutes passed…
The old man looked and saw a big tree.
Under the big tree he saw the young men…
15  They were lying on the ground.
Tired, sweaty and thirsty.
They had no strength to walk.
The old man stopped and facing forward said:
"The wind is old, very old. But is still the wind.
20  I am an old man, very old. But I am still a man…"
The old man was walking through the beautiful sidewalk.
He walked alone and in silence…

Jesus M Bauzo

## Guided writing

1   Write answers to these questions.

   **a**   How do you think the old man felt when the young men made fun of him?

   **b**   How do you think he felt when he caught up with the young men?

   **c**   What do you think the old man meant when he said "The wind is old, very old. But is still the wind. I am an old man, very old. But I am still a man…"?

   **d**   What can we learn from this story?

### Glossary

**ardor (ardour)** enthusiasm
**sidewalk** pavement
**accompanied** kept company with or joined
**mocked** made fun of

- Take on roles in a group
- Write a playscript
- Discuss how the characters talk and act

# Writing a playscript

**2** In small groups, copy and complete the writing frame below to retell the story of the old man's walk. Make sure everyone's ideas in the group are heard.

## Writing frame

| Setting | Character |
|---|---|
| Opening | |
| Build-up | |
| Main event/problem | |
| Resolution | |
| Moral | |

## Your writing

**3** In your groups, discuss how this story could be turned into a playscript.

Use your writing frame to plan a playscript with dialogue and stage directions. Remind yourselves how to set out a playscript with the names of characters on the left, no speech marks and with stage directions in brackets.

You will need a narrator and characters.

- Will you add more characters?
- Will you add new dialogue?
- Will you continue the story?

## Performance

**4** In your group, discuss how to show what the old man is like through his actions and gestures. How will these be different to those of the young men? When you have written and rehearsed it, perform your play for an audience.

# Revise and check ②

## Vocabulary

**1** Write out the sentences below. Underline the adverbial in each sentence.

   **a** He climbed the mountain with great care.

   **b** Last Wednesday, I went to see my grandparents.

   **c** The children kicked the ball over the fence.

   **d** I am sitting very quietly.

**2** Copy and complete these similes and metaphors.

   **a** The biscuit was as hard as _____

   **b** Your room is a _____

   **c** The stars glittered like _____

   **d** The dog slept like _____

## Punctuation

**1** Rewrite the sentence twice so that the reporting clause –
'she announced' – comes in a different place each time.
Remember to check your punctuation.

she announced I have always loved reading ever since I was
given my first science fiction book when I was six.

# Grammar

1 **Rewrite the sentences below using direct speech. Add the correct punctuation.**

   a   Scott told us that it was a brilliant match.

   b   He announced that he was going to start training too.

   c   He said he wanted to be part of the winning team.

   d   He hoped we would all support him and asked us to wish him luck.

2 **Write the sentences below as reported speech and punctuate them correctly.**

   a   "Tell me how you came to be here, Petey," Sophie asked.

   b   "Well," said Petey, "someone rang up from the hospital."

   c   "Go on," said Sophie, "tell me what happened next."

   d   "You are not going to believe me!" said Petey.

3 **Rewrite the text below. Change all the highlighted contractions to full words.**

I'm sorry, I couldn't find the shop, but don't worry. There's a market close by and I'll buy more there. They weren't very expensive. You'll love them! They're bright yellow, like the ones Adam has.

# Spelling

1 **Write the plural of these words:**

   a   wolf

   b   knife

   c   loaf

   d   yourself

   e   shelf

   f   life

2 **Write these words as plurals using the correct rule.**

   a   play

   b   holiday

   c   story

   d   puppy

   e   birthday

   f   party

# 7 It's a small world

## Talk time

Storytelling is an important part of many cultures. For example, the Indigenous Australian people use it to explain about nature and their history.

What stories do you know that explain about your culture?

- Talk about your own and other cultures
- Share stories from other cultures
- Research celebrations in other cultures

# Storytelling around the world

**A** The words listed below (1 to 4) are linked to the culture of the Indigenous Australian people. Match the words to their correct meaning.

**1** Didgeridoo

**2** Dreamtime

**3** Body painting

**4** Uluru

**a** this shows information about a person such as their age and status

**b** a spiritual place in the outback

**c** a musical instrument

**d** when everything was created, according to Indigenous Australian legend

**B** Here are some events celebrated in different cultures.

- Diwali
- Thanksgiving
- Chinese New Year
- Cocuk Bayrami
- Songkran Water Festival
- Eid

What do you know about them? Do some research to find out more about these celebrations. Write one or two sentences about each of them.

**C** What about you?

**1** What do you think is an important feature or celebration in your culture?

**2** What would you include in a children's story about your culture? What characters would you include? Where would it be set? What would its theme or message be?

Make notes about your ideas that you can present, and discuss them.

## In the marketplace

A busy **hubbub** rang out from all over the bustling marketplace. Mr Rashid weaved his way through the crowds. Before he left his shop, he had pinned a notice to a piece
5 of silk fabric hanging by the entrance that read 'Back in ten minutes'.

Abdul was left outside the shop, minding it until his father returned. He sat on a small stool, happy to be helping out during his
10 school holidays.

The **souk** was laden with Middle Eastern **souvenirs** spilling out from tiny stalls on the roadside. Colourful cushions were piled high on the ground, propping up polished
15 brass ornaments and golden jewellery boxes. Hanging above, on long poles, were cashmere shawls and glittering **mosaic** oil lamps. Incense wafted around, smouldering in carved wooden burners, made by local
20 craftsmen, infused with the exotic scents of spices and perfumes known as *oud*.

As shoppers passed by, Abdul tried to guess where they were from. Mostly tourists, he imagined, from foreign places where it was
25 not nearly as hot as it was in his country.

Foreigners, not used to the intense heat, were eager to buy bottles of chilled water to quench their thirst. Abdul noticed a little boy at the drinks' stall opposite. He studied
30 his pale skin and his western clothes, so different to how Abdul looked, with his dark **complexion**, curly brown hair and traditional white robe. Perhaps the boy is English, thought Abdul. The little boy's
35 mother called to him from further down the street. He sauntered over to join her as she approached Mr Rashid's shop.

"Silk scarves?" asked Abdul, as they came nearer. He tried to remember some English
40 words. "Good price," he said. Many times

he had heard his father say this to customers as they bargained over how much a particular item should cost. Nothing in the souk was ever a fixed price.

45 The little boy's mother fingered a piece of woven cloth. She turned as she heard a man approaching. "Come in," welcomed Abdul's father. "I give you good price."

Abdul grinned at the little boy who smiled back, shyly. "Like some dates?" offered
50 Abdul, pointing to a tray of exotic dried fruit and pomegranates. He pulled up another small stool beside him. The little boy nodded and sat down.

### Glossary

**hubbub** chaotic noise caused by a crowd of people

**souk** marketplace or bazaar

**souvenirs** objects kept as a reminder of a holiday

**mosaic** pattern made with pieces of tile or glass

**complexion** natural colour of someone's skin

- Use clues in the story to answer questions
- Tell the story from another character's viewpoint
- Talk about personal experiences

# Comprehension

**A** Here are three different summaries of the extract, below. With a partner, decide which summary is best and why.

1 Mr Rashid often left Abdul to run the stall for him.

2 Abdul liked to make friends with children who shopped at the souk.

3 Abdul learned how to sell fabric from watching his father.

**B** Write answers to these questions, using the text to help you.

1 What did the market smell of?

2 Name six souvenirs that you could buy in the market.

3 Did many local people shop in the market?

4 Why do you think that nothing in the souk was ever a fixed price?

**C** 1 Continue the story by writing a conversation that the two boys might have had at the end of the extract. Would it consist of just words? How else would they have asked each other questions?

2 Imagine you are on holiday. What would you say to someone you had only just met? What food or drink might you offer them? With a partner, imagine that you have never met before and have a conversation with each other.

**?**

Do you know anyone who was born in another country? Perhaps they eat different foods to you or wear different clothes. Do they speak a different language?

# Prepositions and prepositional phrases

- Recognise prepositions and prepositional phrases
- Use prepositional phrases in sentences

A **preposition** is a word that comes before a noun or noun phrase and shows the relationship with that noun or noun phrase.

*Examples:* We drove **under** the railway line, then **past** the shops.

Prepositions often show:

**Time: at** one o'clock          **Place: on** the table

**Direction: to** the shops      **Possession: with** ideas

**Manner: by** car

A **prepositional phrase** includes a preposition and the noun or noun phrase it is linked to. All of the examples above are prepositional phrases.

**A** With a partner, read the paragraph below. Find the five prepositional phrases and list them. Underline each preposition.

> A busy hubbub rang out from all over the bustling marketplace. Mr Rashid weaved his way through the crowds. Before he left his shop, he had pinned a notice to a piece of silk fabric hanging by the entrance that read 'Back in ten minutes'.

**B** Use the four prepositional phrases below to write four full sentences. Each prepositional phrase should come at the **end** of the sentence.

*Example:* I woke up **during the night**.

1  during the night          3  by the sea

2  behind the house        4  since the weekend

**C** Rewrite your sentences in activity B, putting the prepositional phrases at the start of each sentence. Remember to add a comma after the prepositional phrase.

*Example:* During the night**,** I heard a strange sound.

- Identify subordinate clauses and main clauses
- Use commas to separate clauses

# Subordinate clauses

Some multi-clause sentences have a **main clause** – that makes sense on its own – and a **subordinate clause**, which doesn't make sense on its own. Look at the multi-clause sentences below.

| Main clause | Subordinate clause |
| --- | --- |
| She answered her phone | while doing her homework. |
| She answered her phone | although she didn't want to. |

The subordinate clause can come before the main clause. This gives it more emphasis. A comma is used to separate the two clauses.

*Example:* While doing her homework, she answered her phone.

**A** Rewrite these sentences so that the subordinate clause comes first. Remember to use a comma to separate the two clauses.

1 There was a knock at the door as he was reading the paper.

2 You should plan your writing before starting to write.

3 Abdul tried to speak to the boy although his English was not good.

Sometimes commas are used to show that extra information has been added to the middle of a sentence. This is called an embedded clause and it doesn't make sense on its own.

**Ellen Singer, who is ten years old, won the poetry competition.**

*Notice the comma on either side.*

**Language tip**
A subordinate clause always starts with a subordinating conjunction. *Examples:* **who, while, although, if, when.**

**B** Rewrite the sentences below to include the information in the brackets. Remember to add two commas.

1 My father is a good sportsman. (who plays football and swims)

2 Makoto is always falling off his bike. (the boy who lives down the road)

3 The rain is flooding the road. (which is coming down heavily)

113

● Read a story set in a particular culture

This story is set in Tanzania. Saruni has been saving his money to buy a bicycle so that he can carry heavy goods to the market. His father is helping him to learn to ride.

## My Rows and Piles of Coins

After several more lessons **Murete** let me ride on my own while he shouted instructions. "Eyes up, arms straight, keep pedalling, slow down!" I enjoyed the breeze on my face, the pedals turning smoothly under my feet, and most of all,
5 **Yeyo's** proud smile as she watched me ride. How surprised she would be to see my new bicycle! And how grateful she would be when I used it to help her on market days!

The heavy March rains came. The ground became so muddy, nobody went to market. Instead, I helped Yeyo with
10 house **chores**. When it wasn't raining, I helped Murete on the coffee farm. Whenever I could, I practised riding Murete's bicycle.

It stopped raining in June. Our harvest – maize and peas, sweet potatoes, vegetables, and fruits – was so big, we went to market on Saturdays *and* Wednesdays. My money box grew heavier and heavier.

15     I emptied the box,
        arranged the coins in piles
        and the piles in rows.
        Then I counted the coins
        and thought about the bicycle
20     I would buy.

After a few days, I grew confident enough to try to ride a loaded bicycle. With Murete's help, I strapped a giant **pumpkin** on the carrier behind me. When I attempted to pedal, the bicycle wobbled so dangerously that Murete, alongside me, had to grab it.

25 "All right, Saruni, the load is too heavy for you," he said, and I got off.  Mounting the bicycle to ride back to the house, he sighed wearily. "And hard on my bones, which are getting too old for pedalling."

I practised daily with smaller loads, and slowly I learned
30 to ride a loaded bicycle. No more pushing the squeaky old wheelbarrow, I thought. I would ride with my load tall and proud on my bicycle – just like Murete!

From *My Rows and Piles of Coins* by Tololwa M. Mollel

### Glossary

**Murete** Maasai term of affection for an older member of the family
**Yeyo** Maasai for mother
**chores** jobs
**pumpkin** large round fruit with a hard skin and orange flesh

# Comprehension

Write answers to these questions, using the extract to
help you.

1 Which two statements about Saruni are true?

    **a** He kept falling off when he was riding a bicycle.

    **b** He wanted a bicycle so that he could help his mother.

    **c** He needed a bicycle to go to school.

    **d** He wanted the bicycle he was buying to be a surprise
    to his mother.

2 What crops did Saruni's family grow?

**B** Using the extract, write answers to these questions and then
compare your answers with a partner's.

1 How long did the rains last?

2 The writer repeats lines 15–20 two other times in different
parts of the story. Suggest a reason for this.

3 From whose point of view is the story written?
Explain your answer.

**C** Saruni practised riding the bike whenever he could.
With a partner, talk about what sort of things might
have stopped Saruni from practising.

- Find details in the story
  to answer questions
- Use clues in the story to
  answer questions
- Discuss what motivates
  characters

**Stretch zone**

Look back at the extract *In
the marketplace* on page 110.
Make a list of the similarities
and differences between
these two stories. This might
involve the characters, the
style of the language and
the story's message.

# Getting the verbs right

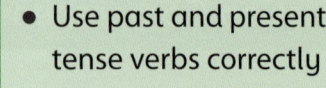

**A** Read the text below. The writer has used the wrong form of the verbs. Rewrite the text, correcting the verbs (in bold). Read your new text aloud to a partner to check it sounds right.

Slowly, very slowly, Ali **approach** the old, wooden door. What **were** on the other side? Fumbling, he **insert** the key in the lock, the thick darkness of the night **make** it difficult. Eventually, it **click**. He **make** the first turn. A second. A third. Bit by bit, it **were** turning, turning, turning, the noise **echo** through the cold night air. What would he **be finding** on the other side?

**B** Rewrite these sentences, putting the verbs in the correct tense.

1 I was sorry that I had _____ the vase, because I _____ it. (smash/like)

2 He _____ very slowly all the way home, as the windscreen had _____. (drive/break)

3 The gardener _____ her lunch, then _____ the vegetable patch. (eat/dig)

**C** Sometimes people speak in non-standard English. This means that the verb and subject don't match. The sentences below are in non-standard English. Rewrite each sentence in standard English. The first one has been done for you.

1 I ain't bothered. **I'm not bothered.**

2 She don't care.

3 I'm gonna do it.

4 I wanna do it.

**?**

Can you think of any situations where non-standard English is used? When should you use standard English and when is it acceptable to use non-standard English?

> • Use synonyms in your own writing

# Synonyms

**Synonyms** are words which have similar meanings. **Horrible**, **nasty** and **disgusting** are synonyms for the word 'bad'.

Some verbs, such as **went**, **ate** and **said** are very common and do not give the reader much detail. It is better to replace them in your writing with more interesting synonyms.

**A** Look at the difference between the verbs in these sentences.

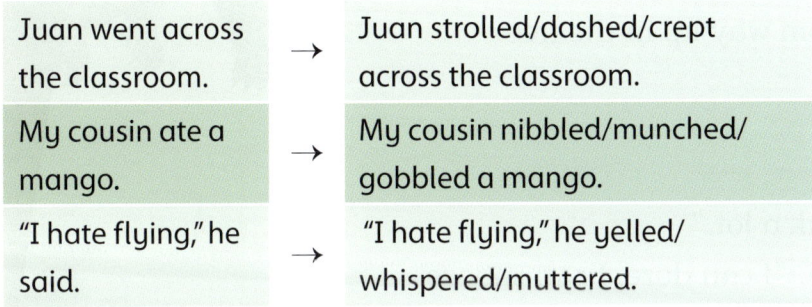

| Juan **went** across the classroom. | → | Juan strolled/dashed/crept across the classroom. |
| My cousin **ate** a mango. | → | My cousin nibbled/munched/ gobbled a mango. |
| "I hate flying," he **said**. | → | "I hate flying," he yelled/ whispered/muttered. |

Rewrite the sentences below, replacing the words in bold with a synonym from the box.

> attached    assisted    solo    swayed

**1** Murete let me ride **alone**.

**2** When it rained, I **helped** with the chores.

**3** Murete **strapped** a pumpkin to the bicycle.

**4** "The bicycle **wobbled** as I rode it down the road," said Saruni.

**B** A new girl, Anna, arrives in the classroom. In the writing below, the verbs show her to be shy and quiet. Change these verbs so that Anna becomes bold and confident.

Anna **crept** into the classroom.
"Where do I sit, Sir?" she **muttered**.

"Over there, Anna," replied the teacher, pointing at an empty chair.

Anna **shuffled** across the room.
"I hope this is the right chair," she **whispered**.

● Read a traditional story

This story is about a young wombat who gets lost and is unable to find his mother. He meets some animals and a boy, all of whom believe they are superior to Wombat. The last one he meets is Koala...

## Wombat Goes Walkabout

It was baking hot now, and Wombat shuffled into the shade of a great eucalyptus tree. He hoped his mother might be there. But she wasn't.

"Who are you?" called Koala from way up in the tree
5  above him.

"I'm Wombat," said Wombat.

"And what can you do?"

"Not much. I dig a lot and I think a lot."

"That's nothing," laughed Koala. "I can doze, I can snooze,
10  I can snore. Look at me." And very soon she was dozing and snoozing away high up in her eucalyptus tree. By now Wombat was very, very tired. So he lay down in the shade and sang himself to sleep.

When Wombat woke up, he looked around for his mother.
15  But she still wasn't there. "I know," he thought. "I'll climb the highest hill I can find. Surely I'll be able to see her then." So that's what he did. He climbed and he climbed and he climbed.

When he reached the top he looked about him. Everywhere he looked there were lots of cackling kookaburras, hopping
20  wallabies, swinging possums, hunting boys, scampering emus, and dozing koalas. But no matter how hard he looked, he just couldn't see his mother anywhere.

But he did see something else. He saw smoke. He saw fire. It was leaping from tree to tree. It was coming straight
25  towards him. Wombat thought hard, very hard. Suddenly he knew what to do. He ran down the hill as fast as he could, and began to dig. He dug and he dug and he dug.

Then Kookaburra came by, and
30  Wallaby and Possum and Emu and Boy and Koala.
"Fire!" they all cried.
"Run, run, you silly

- Recognise language devices used by the writer
- Use the extract as a model for writing your own story
- Write from the viewpoint of another character

Wombat. Fire! Fire!"

35 But Wombat just went on digging.

"What are you doing?" they asked.

"I'm digging," replied Wombat."And I'm thinking too."

"What are you thinking?" they cried.

"I'm thinking that fire burns faster than you can run

40 or fly or hop or swing. And I'm thinking that there's plenty of room down in my hole if you want to join me. We'll be quite safe."

They took one look at all the crackling fire and all the billowing smoke. One look was all they needed.

From *Wombat Goes Walkabout* by
Michael Morpurgo

## Comprehension

**A** **Write answers to these questions, using the extract to help you.**

1 Find three examples of repetition.

2 Give three examples of short sentences. What effect do they have?

**B** **Write answers to these questions.**

1 Look at the extract. Think of synonyms for the following words used in the extract.

**a** cackling (line 19)

**b** came by (line 29)

**c** hole (line 41)

2 What picture is the writer giving in line 17 by repeating some words, in 'He climbed and he climbed and he climbed'?

3 The writer is talking about the animals and the boy when he writes, 'One look was all they needed.' All they needed to do what?

4 What moral is the writer teaching us in this story?

**C** **Research native Australian animals and write a short story about one. Write it from the viewpoint of your chosen animal.**

- Recognise homophones
- Use homophones correctly

# Homophones

**Homophones** are words that sound the same but have different meanings. They are often spelt differently, which can be confusing.

**A** **They're**, **their** and **there** are three words that sound the same.

Try to remember their different meanings:

- **they're** means 'they are'
- **their** means 'belonging to them'
- **there** means 'that place'.

**Copy and complete the following sentences.**

1 Rows and piles of coins were _____ on the table.

2 Rich people travel in _____ limousines.

3 I think _____ too busy to notice me.

4 _____ going into the scary old cafe, but I don't know why.

**B** **Where** and **wear** are two words with different meaning.

Try to remember how they are different:

- If it refers to a place, write **where**.
- If it is to do with clothes, write **wear**.

**Copy and complete the following sentences.**

1 _____ are you going tomorrow?

2 What are you going to _____ to the party?

3 _____ have you put your orange scarf?

4 _____ are you going? Will you need to _____ your scarf?

**Stretch zone**

Think of ways to remember the difference between **who's** and **whose**, and **it's** and **its**. Can you think of ways of remembering other pairs of homophones?

- Try different ways to remember difficult spellings
- Share your ideas in a group

# Learn difficult spellings

 **A** Here are some words that can be difficult to spell.

> ache    international    beautiful    foreign    ocean
> favourite    success    valuable    medicine    balloon
> material    envelope    technical    chocolate

1 Read, say and listen to the words above with a partner.

2 Write the words in alphabetical order.

3 Write a definition for each word. Use a dictionary or an online tool.

**Here are some tips for remembering the spellings:**

Write the word out and make the difficult letters large or different.

suCCess                    bEAUtiful

Break the word into syllables or chunks.

mat-er-i-al                tech-ni-cal

Find a word inside the word or draw a picture to help you.

There is a **ball** in **balloon**

There is **our** in **favourite**.

Check for a spelling rule.

**Whiz** ends in a consonant, **z**, and has a short vowel sound before it,

so double the consonant when **-ed** is added.

whiz → whizzed

**B** In small groups, think of ways to remember the spellings for all the words at the top of the page. Use the tips in the box above.

*Example:* There is a **gate** in **navigate**

- Read a story set in a particular culture

Here is more of the story of Saruni and his quest for a bicycle. He is disappointed because the money he has worked hard to save is not enough to buy the bicycle he dreamed of. When his mother asks what is wrong, Saruni explains that he had been saving his money, thirty-five shillings and fifty cents, to buy a bicycle in order to help her carry her goods to market.

## My Rows and Piles of Coins

The next afternoon, the sound of a **pikipiki** filled the air, **tuk-tuk-tuk-tuk-tuk**. I came out of the house and stared in astonishment. **Murete** was perched on an orange motorbike.

He cut the engine and dismounted. Then, chuckling at my
5  excited questions about the *pikipiki*, he headed into the house.

When Murete came out, **Yeyo** was with him, and he was wheeling his bicycle. "I want to sell this to you. For thirty shillings and fifty cents." He winked at me.

Surprised, I stared at Murete. How did he know about my
10  secret money box? I hadn't told him anything.

Then, suddenly, I realized the wonderful thing that had just happened. "My bicycle, I have my very own bicycle!" I said, and it didn't matter at all that it wasn't decorated with red and blue. Within moments, I had brought Murete
15  my money box.

Murete gave Yeyo the box. Yeyo, in turn, gave it to me. Puzzled, I looked from Yeyo to Murete and to Yeyo again. "You're giving it… back to me?"

Yeyo smiled. "It's a reward for all your
20  help to us."

"Thank you, thank you!" I cried, gleefully.

The next Saturday, my load sat tall and proud on my bicycle, which I walked importantly to market. I wasn't riding it
25  because Yeyo could never have kept up.

Looking over at Yeyo, I wished she didn't have to carry such a big load on her head…

From *My Rows and Piles of Coins*
by Tololwa M. Mollel

**Glossary**

**pikipiki** Swahili for motorcycle or motorbike

**tuk-tuk-tuk-tuk-tuk** the sound of an engine in Maasai

**Murete** a Maasai term of affection for an older member of the family

**Yeyo** Maasai for mother

# Comprehension

- Summarise the plot of the story
- Discuss Saruni's character
- Predict what might happen next in the story

**A** Write these parts of the extract in the correct order.

**1** Saruni paid Murete for the bicycle.

**2** Murete went to fetch the bicycle.

**3** The bicycle was stacked high.

**4** Murete and Yeyo returned the money.

**B** Write answers to these questions, using the extract to help you.

**1** Which of the following words would you use to describe Saruni's character?

> ambitious    selfish    arrogant
> foolish    determined    considerate

What synonyms can you think of for the words you chose?

**2** List some words and phrases to describe the setting in this extract and the one on page 114.

**3** Describe how Saruni's feelings change during this extract.

**C** What do you think?

The extract ends with Saruni wishing his mother didn't have to carry such a heavy load on her head. Think about what you know of Saruni's character. What do you think he might do next to help his mother? Discuss your ideas with a partner.

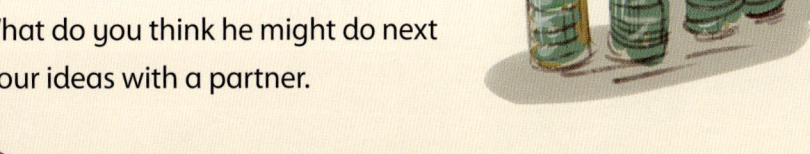

Saruni is keen to help his mother to get their harvest to the market. Many children help their families. In what ways do you help your family? Do children have a duty to help their family in any way that they can? Explain your views carefully.

- Use an exciting story as a model for own writing
- Use suitable writing techniques for the type of story

# Writing an exciting story

Writers use techniques to make their stories exciting for readers.

For example, instead of just describing what is happening, a writer uses conversation between characters to bring the story 'alive'.

## Model writing

1 Read the extract below. Mohamed and Jon have spent the last few days enjoying the local festival celebrations. Now the fun is over, they have nothing to entertain them. The coloured notes at the side explain the techniques the writer has used to excite the reader's interest so that they want to read on.

Action and movement add interest for the reader.

Adverbs add detail to help the reader imagine what the characters say and do.

Strong, precise verbs explain what is happening.

Bad weather and darkness are included to create an atmosphere.

Notice where the commas have been placed!

"Oh, I'm so bored," moaned Mohamed, throwing himself down on the bed. "Nothing exciting ever happens round here any more."

"Yeah," Jon agreed, flopping back wearily in the
5 chair opposite him. "I don't want to spend the rest of the summer break hanging around, getting bored."

They both sat for a minute in silence, staring morosely at the rain battering against the window. It was only 7 o'clock, but already the sky was dark
10 and forbidding.

Suddenly, Mohamed jumped up. "I know, let's go and explore the old cafe on the main road. I've heard the door has been left open. What about it?"

"Yes, yes!" Jon shouted excitedly. "Why not? Let's
15 get going!"

**2** Read part two of the story. Find examples of the techniques listed in the coloured boxes in the story. Copy and complete the table below, using the examples you have found.

The use of strong, precise verbs that explain what happens

Use of a rhetorical question

Repetition

Use of adverbs

Use of commas to separate phrases and clauses

Use of simile

Use of ellipses

Weather and noise

As they approached the old cafe, they began to feel scared. Very scared indeed. Why on earth had they come here? The night was pitch black, the road was deserted. Moaning eerily, the wind whipped angrily
5  around their ankles, like a fierce dog.

Jon shuddered. "Perhaps we should go back. It looks like—"

"No," Mohamed interrupted, not wanting to show him that he was scared too. "Just a quick look, and
10  then we'll go home. It won't take a minute."

What was left of the old cafe was now in full view. Run down, dirty, neglected, its windows broken and torn blinds flapping in the cold night wind. Clouds covered the moon. A sudden bang came from behind
15  them. They both shivered. Nervously, very nervously, they both crept towards the open front door...

| Technique | Example from part 2 |
|---|---|
| Strong, precise verbs | |
| Rhetorical question | |
| Repetition | |
| Adverbs | |
| Commas to separate clauses and phrases | |
| Simile | |
| Ellipses | |
| Extreme weather | |
| Sudden noise | |

## Your writing

**3** Write the opening of your own exciting story. Use the techniques you have identified in the model text to add excitement to your own writing.

Part 1 Begin with two friends who see something mysterious and decide to go and investigate.

Part 2 Describe how they creep towards the place but stop just before the door or gate.

Swap your work with a partner. Check that you are both using the techniques to create an exciting story.

125

"**Don't raise your voice, improve your argument.**"
Desmond Tutu

## Talk time

1 Look at the pictures and list all the different methods of persuading people to do, think or buy something.

2 How do you think you might be persuaded by these methods?

3 What methods do you use to try to persuade other people to do things or to agree with you?

- Discuss how people can be persuaded
- Identify the features of persuasive writing
- Use persuasive language

# Language that persuades

**A** What would you say to someone to persuade them to:

**a** buy a vacuum cleaner

**b** go on a holiday to the South Pole

**c** not build a multi-storey car park next to your house

**d** do your homework for you?

**B 1** Read the phrases below. They are from newspapers, leaflets, adverts, letters, emails and TV.

**a** Get the Best!

**b** I hope you agree.

**c** This is a good idea because…

**d** In tests, 90% of shoppers chose it!

**e** Do you really want this **monstrosity** on your doorstep?

**f** You say that nothing can be done, but if you do this…

**g** You'll never have to work hard again!

**h** Only feed your favourite **feline** fishy flakes

**i** He is an outstanding candidate

With a partner, discuss where you might find each phrase and what it might be persuading people to do.

**2** Match each of the phrases above to one of the features of persuasive writing below. Only use each feature once.

**1** Includes a counter argument to show the reader they were incorrect

**2** Addresses the reader directly

**3** Factual information included

**4** Alliteration to grab the reader's attention

**5** Promises a better life if you use or do it

**6** Memorable slogan

**7** Use of powerful adjectives

**8** Rhetorical questions

**9** You have evidence to support your main point

> **Glossary**
>
> **monstrosity** a dreadful or shocking thing
> **feline** to do with cats
> **memorable** easy to remember

# FirstNews

*FirstNews* is a weekly newspaper aimed at 7–14 year olds. It aims to present **current events** alongside entertainment, sport and computer games. It is published on Fridays and is read by over two million children every week all over the
5 world. The newspaper was started in May 2006.

**Bursting with content!**

Every issue is packed from cover to cover with the latest stories about world and **home affairs**, the environment, sports, entertainment and puzzles, all selected to engage
10 and inspire its readers.

**Meet two of the *FirstNews* team**

The *FirstNews* team includes **editors**, writers, designers and many more.

Rich is the Design Manager, which means that he has to
15 make the paper look good and add all the pictures. That isn't always an easy job.

Ben is the Website and **Marketing Assistant**. Ben is a big fan of all things entertainment – film, TV, magazines and computer games. He loves writing, hanging out with
20 friends and visiting different places.

### Get *FirstNews* delivered every Friday!

*FirstNews* is the ONLY weekly newspaper for young people. It is now the widest-read children's publication with over 2 million readers every week!

*FirstNews* journalists provide up-to-date, **insightful** and **dynamic** articles on a range of subjects from entertainment to politics, sport to science which will be really interesting to students aged 7–14.

Treat a special child in your life to a *FirstNews* subscription and they will discover a read which is vibrantly presented, thought-provoking, intelligent – and fun! Don't miss out – subscribe NOW.

## Glossary

**current events** news about things happening now

**home affairs** events that happen in the country where the paper is based

**editors** people who prepare books, newspapers and magazines for publication

**marketing assistant** person who helps to tell people about a product

**insightful** understanding the truth about things

**dynamic** lively

- Understand the difference between facts and opinions
- Compare the features of news reports and adverts

# Comprehension

**A** Read the statements below. With a partner, decide which are true and which are false.

1 *FirstNews* is a monthly paper for adults.

2 Each issue always has a sports section.

3 The very first issue was published last Friday.

4 It has over 100,000 readers each week.

**B** Find answers to these questions.

1 Read the statements below. Which is the best description of the text on the website?

   **a** It contains only facts.

   **b** It contains mostly facts.

   **c** It contains mostly opinions.

   **d** It contains half facts and half opinions.

2 The information in both texts is about the newspaper *FirstNews* but the style of language is different. One is a news feature report and one is a persuasive advert.

Find and write out two phrases from each text to show how they are different.

3 Would you want to buy *FirstNews*? If so, what persuaded you?

**C** Discuss your answers to the questions below with a partner.

1 What job would you like to have on a newspaper?

2 Which features of a newspaper do you think are the most interesting?

**?** "Good news stories should contain only facts and not opinions." Do you agree or disagree? Explain your opinion to a partner.

# Opposites and prefixes

- Add prefixes to root words to make their opposites
- Understand the meaning of more prefixes
- Use a dictionary to check meanings

*FirstNews* claims to be really interesting to students aged 7–14. If you didn't like it, it would be 'uninteresting'. The prefix **un-** is used to make the opposite of interesting.

**A 1** Create new words by adding **un-**.

> able    believable    acceptable    attached    aware
> certain    breakable    comfortable    clean
> convinced    fasten    lucky    noticed    real
> safe    wanted    reasonable    truthful    well

**2** Use six of the words above in sentences that might persuade people to do something.
*Example:* This product has unbelievable cleaning power, so buy it now!

The prefixes **dis-**, **in-**, **il-**, **ir-** and **im-** also mean 'not'.
*Examples:* **dis**appoint, **in**justice, **il**legal, **ir**regular, **im**polite

**B 1** Attach the right prefix to the root words below. Be careful, as it is easy to get them mixed up. Check a dictionary first!

> __ possible    __ belief    __ legible
> __ rational    __ visible

**2** Find two more words beginning with each of these prefixes.

**C** With a partner, find out what these prefixes mean:

> sub-    auto-    trans-    super-    micro-

Use a dictionary and list three words that start with each of these prefixes.

# Shades of meaning and comparisons

**Synonyms** (words with similar meanings) can be ordered according to how strong they are.

*Example:* happy → thrilled → ecstatic

- Jo is **happy** that her article is being published.
- Jo is **thrilled** that she has been asked to write more articles.
- Jo is **ecstatic** that she has been asked to become the editor.

Compared to **happy**, **thrilled** is a stronger word and **ecstatic** is even stronger.

**A** Fill the gaps in the sentences below with the strongest word.

1 "Our vacuum cleaners are _____." (great, good, fantastic)

2 The parents had _____ ideas about how to reduce the traffic. (quite a few, loads of, some)

3 When the teacher asked us to help save the polar bears, we were _____. (enthusiastic, keen, willing)

**B** Write out these synonyms in order of intensity, starting with the weakest. Compare your order to your partner's.

1 angry, furious, cross

2 bite, gobble, nibble

3 soaked, damp, wet, drenched

We can make **comparisons** using adjectives.

To compare two things or people, use the **comparative** form with **-er** or '**more**...' *Examples:* short**er, more** famous

To compare three or more things or people, use the **superlative** form with **-est** or '**most**...' *Examples:* small**est**, **most** expensive

**C** Copy and complete this table.

| adjective | comparative | superlative |
|---|---|---|
| strong | | strongest |
| | | funniest |
| beautiful | | |

# WANT TO SAVE A LIFE?

# THEN WEAR A CYCLING HELMET

You think you're a good cyclist? You don't think you need a helmet? This boy was a good cyclist but he still got knocked off his bike! Lucky for him he was wearing a helmet or he could have had a serious head injury! It doesn't matter how good a cyclist **you** are, it's other people on the roads you have to worry about! Good cyclists can still get knocked off their bikes so wise up and ride safe – **wear a helmet**!

# Comprehension

**A** Write answers to these questions, using the poster to support your answers.

1 What is this poster trying to persuade you to do?

2 Whose life is the poster trying to save?

3 If you are a good cyclist, how safe are you on a bicycle? Explain your answer.

4 What is meant by 'wise up'?

**B** Write answers to these questions.

1 What is the first thing you notice about the poster?

2 Why do you think there is a child in the picture rather than an adult?

3 Give some examples of words and phrases that are used in the poster to alarm you.

4 What effect does using the words 'knocked off' rather than 'fell off' have on the reader's feelings about cycling safety?

5 Which of the following features of persuasive advertising does the writer use in this poster?

   a Only positive things are mentioned

   b Eye-catching picture     c Offers discounts

   d Questions to make the reader think

   e Friendly     f Repeats phrases

**C** Discuss these questions in a small group.

1 How effective do you think this poster is at encouraging people to wear cycling helmets? Which words and phrases in the poster are most effective at persuading you to wear a cycling helmet?

2 What advice would you give to someone who says they are a careful cyclist and won't have an accident?

# Idioms

**Idioms** are common sayings. Their meaning is figurative – which is different from what the words mean literally (exactly as stated). The idiom used in the *FirstNews* extract, 'hanging out with friends', means Ben likes to see his friends, not actually 'hang' anywhere.

**A** Many idioms would be absurd if the words were used literally. From the list below, choose two idioms that would be absurd if taken literally. Draw these literal images. (The first one has been drawn for you.)

1 The spelling test was a piece of cake.
(a task that was completed very easily)

2 He visits us only once in a blue moon. (rarely)

3 The new coat cost an arm and a leg.
(was very expensive)

4 The child's behaviour was driving me up the wall.
(was annoying me very much)

**B** 1 Many idioms use pairs of words. Choose the correct missing words to finish the phrases.

> square   dogs   neck   riches

a The two horses were running neck and _____ .

b We won the competition fair and _____ .

c She has gone from rags to _____ almost overnight.

d The weather was terrible; it was raining cats and _____ .

2 Match the meanings below to the idioms above.

fairly, with no cheating

very heavy rain          go from being poor to rich

exactly even

# Compound words and spelling strategies

- Break down compound words to help learn spellings
- Use a dictionary to check meanings and spellings

**Compound words** are made up of two (or more) words.

Each word makes sense on its own, but when joined together they make a different word.

*Example:* lady (woman) + bird (flying animal) = ladybird (small, red insect)

Compound words are easier to spell if you break them up into separate words.

**A** Add words from the table to the gaps below to make compound word strings. The first one has been done for you.

| play | back | fast | light |
|------|------|------|-------|
| news | pack | bed | paper |
| break | table | spoon | house |
| work | side | time | day |

1 news / <u>paper</u> / back / <u>pack</u> = newspaper / paperback / backpack

2 birth / _____ / break / _____ =

3 day / _____ / house / _____ =

4 bed / _____ / table / _____ =

**B** Write three sentences with at least two compound words in each sentence.

**C** Find other compound words in books in the classroom. With a partner, test your spelling of these words. Remember to break them into two words to help you. Explain what the words mean and check your definitions in a dictionary.

# Advertising campaign

In groups, you are going to plan an advertising campaign for a new variety of biscuit. First, imagine your new type of biscuit. Make sure everyone in your group has a chance to explain their ideas.

- Make notes in a planning frame
- Take on roles in a group task
- Add your own ideas to discussions
- Proof-read, check and improve work
- Prepare a presentation

## A Planning frame

On a large piece of paper, note the group's ideas about the following:

- Description – what makes your biscuit different to rival biscuits?
- Audience – who will eat your biscuit? Is this different from who will buy it?
- What do they currently buy? Why should they buy your biscuit instead?

## Your advertising

- Discuss the best places to advertise your biscuit.
- What media will you use? TV? Radio? Magazines? Posters? Internet? A combination is best.
- Make sure everyone in the group has a role, such as designing artwork, making a poster, researching on the Internet, making notes, gathering everything together, script writing.
- Discuss the advantages and disadvantages of advertising media. Then copy and complete the table.

|  | Advantages | Disadvantages |
| --- | --- | --- |
| Magazines | You can target an audience that has a particular interest, for example through food magazines. |  |
| Television |  | Expensive |
| Posters | A lot of people will see them if put in busy public places. |  |
| Internet |  |  |
| Social media |  |  |

## Persuasive language

Choose your words carefully to get people's attention.
Use the words and phrases below in some sentences to
advertise your biscuit.

| biscuit | cheaper | exclusive |
|---|---|---|
| special offer | 3 for 2 | brilliant |

Think about the features of persuasive advertising
(see page 127, activity B2) and include these in your 'ad campaign'.

### B  Writing

When you are ready, write and draw your adverts, posters, scripts,
etc. You can use computers, the Internet, photographs, drawings and
whatever other methods you want to create your advertisements.

### Rewriting

Advertising is always checked on a small group of people before
being seen by the public. Check each other's work in the group; then
test it out on friends and family.

### C  Going live

Now present your campaign to the rest of the class.

As a class, discuss who presented the most persuasive
advertising campaign.

# Personal pronouns

> **Personal pronouns** refer to a person or a thing without naming it. So, rather than saying 'Nimish' or 'the girl', we can use the pronouns **he** and **she**.

**A** These sentences don't sound right. With a partner, talk about which pronouns you would change to nouns to make the meaning clearer.

1 Iona showed her mother the donkey at the rescue centre. She was hairy and needed a bath.

2 The police officers waited at the airport for the shipment of stolen jewels to arrive. They were hidden in shoe boxes.

3 The hikers saw a herd of sheep in the distance. They were wearing strong walking boots.

**B** Pick out the personal pronouns in the sentences below and say which nouns they refer to.

*Example:* Fatima and Ahmed picked some apricots. They found them in a garden.
(Fatima and Ahmed = they; apricots = them)

1 When Mr and Mrs Smith sent Raphael a new bag he wrote to thank them for it.

2 Philippe had not seen Angelique's new car. He asked her to show it to him.

**C** Rewrite the following sentences, replacing the underlined words with personal pronouns.

1 Jasmin met <u>Javier and Alan</u>.

2 Mary met <u>Nasreen's grandfather</u>.

3 <u>Leticia and I</u> met Angela.

4 <u>Sandeep and Jamelia</u> met Hilary.

5 Amelia and Belen met <u>Hilary and me</u>.

# Possessive pronouns

**Possessive pronouns** are pronouns that show ownership.

*Examples:*   **Yours** is over in the corner.

That chocolate is **mine**.

**A** Pick out the possessive pronouns in the sentences below. There are two in each sentence.

1  That book is mine, not yours.

2  Ours is way over there, so where are yours?

3  Everyone has different coloured shoes. Yours are black, hers are green.

4  Here is your poster. Ours is over there. His is on the wall in the corridor.

5  I found my key and you found yours, but Mary couldn't find hers.

6  All the television adverts were good, but his and hers were the best.

7  This house is mine, but that one across the street is theirs.

**B** Write four sentences, using different possessive pronouns.

**C** As possessive pronouns show who owns things, they are often used in disagreements and arguments!

Two children are arguing about who a book belongs to. Write their conversation!

**Language tip**

Remember that the possessive pronouns are **mine, yours, his, hers, its, ours, theirs**.

Note that the word 'his' can also be used as a possessive determiner.

*Examples:* That is **his** book. (possessive determiner)

That book is **his**. (possessive pronoun)

139

- Identify facts and opinions
- Write a newspaper article
- Use the model text to help organise your writing

# A newspaper article

**A** Read the six steps below, which explain how to structure a news article.

1 Write a headline that sums up the story and grabs the reader's attention.
2 Introduce the topic, explaining the headline and giving facts and figures.
3 Involve the reader by including a quotation from someone at the scene.
4 Develop the story, explaining what happened next.
5 Describe people's responses to the latest action with quotations.
6 Conclude the story in a positive way.

Now read the paragraphs (a to f) below. They are from a newspaper article but are in the wrong order! With a partner, decide on the correct order of these paragraphs. Use steps 1 to 6 above to help you.

**a)** More chickens mean poor families have more birds to sell, raising money to buy food, or pay school fees. "We seem to have struck lucky with this idea!" say the advisers, who have now helped more than 3,700 families.

**b)** "We need to take drastic action. We can't go on like this!" said one desperate farmer.

**c)** "At first I thought it was a joke, but the chicks move about freely within the compound while the hawk is up in the trees, and he has never taken any since I tried it," says one farmer.

**d)** The farmers were visited by an adviser from the UK and were told to try a new and creative method. They dyed the birds pink and purple with a common antiseptic called Gentian Violet. The hawks took no notice of the brightly coloured birds!

**e)** Farmers in Tanzania are dyeing their chickens pink and purple to stop hungry hawks from eating them. Chickens are worth about $5 each and in Tanzania some farmers earn no more than $10 a month. One farmer lost 36 chickens in a month – that is more than he earns in a year!

**f)** Farmers in Tanzania paint chickens pink and purple!

Article by Jan Walter

**B** Find the verbs used in the newspaper article on page 140. List them according to their tense. You could copy the lists started below. Do not include verbs from quotations.

- **Past tenses:** lost, _____
- **Present tenses:** paint, are dyeing, _____
- **Present perfect:** have helped, _____

**C** Write a news article about farmers protecting their animals. Follow the six steps given on page 140. Use the notes below that a journalist made in Namibia, Africa.

Your article should try to persuade more people in Namibia to keep guard dogs instead of killing endangered cheetahs.

### Notes

- fewer cattle deaths
- farmers keeping guard dogs in Namibia – stop cheetahs eating their animals
- last year, 1 farmer lost 12 sheep + 10 goats
- "need to act to protect our animals"
- adviser: keep guard dogs with the herds 24 hours a day. Cheetahs afraid of big guard dogs
- "Cheetahs don't come near our cattle; they go off and hunt deer instead", "We don't have to kill cheetahs (endangered species)" Number of cheetahs in Namibia – stopped falling
- "Good idea!" "Very happy!" 200 working dogs in guard dog programme. Farmers get help with dog care and training

- Read a persuasive letter
- Write a persuasive letter

# Persuasive letters and leaflets

The oil industry in the Delta region of Nigeria causes a lot of pollution. Villagers find it difficult to grow food. The pollution is also bad for their health. The villagers want the oil company to stop polluting their land. The village chief, James Otunde, wrote a letter of complaint to the Managing Director of Southern Oil.

These villagers cannot grow vegetables any more or catch fish because of oil pollution.

Delta Council Buildin
PO Box 9500
Lagos

Mr M Danfodio
Southern Oil Company
Harbour Road, Back Bay

6 May, 2015

Dear Mr Danfodio,

<u>Pollution at Back Bay</u>

I am writing to inform you that the oil wells in Back Bay are still polluting our rivers and killing the fish. Oil is flooding the palm forests and the trees are dying. This is the third letter which we have sent. You have not replied.

The residents of Back Bay are going to take legal action and your company will be hearing from our lawyer shortly. They are also starting a campaign against your company.

I await your reply.

Yours sincerely,

James Otunde (Village Chief)

1 Use the information James Otunde has given, plus the information at the top of the page, to write your own persuasive letter to the Southern Oil Company.

Think about these questions before you start writing your letter.

- Who is your audience?
- What is the purpose of the letter?
- What should you include in the first paragraph?
- What should you include in the next paragraph?
- What should be included in the final paragraph?

## Guided writing

- Carry out research and make notes
- Write a persuasive leaflet and poster
- Use the model text to help you write persuasive language
- Make your viewpoint clear

2   Research an endangered animal (such as the Indian tiger or the mountain gorilla).

3   Plan, write and design a persuasive leaflet that can be sent out to lots of people. Explain the threat to this animal and then suggest ideas for saving the animal from extinction. List the problems and suggested solutions clearly.

- Include facts, powerful and emotive words, rhetorical questions.
- Support your main points with evidence.
- Use repetition for emphasis.
- Ask questions to make the audience think.
- Be enthusiastic.
- Include photographs in the leaflet.

4   Design a poster to save the animal. Write a slogan – a phrase that people will remember.

The mountain gorilla is an endangered species. There are fewer than 800 left in the wild.

143

# 9 A great performance

> "Make your poems sing, whisper, shout and float."
> Michael Rosen

## Talk time

1 What are the people doing in the pictures?

2 What performances have you done in front of an audience?

- Talk about performances you have seen or been in
- Clap the rhythm of a poem
- Perform a poem

## Alligator Problem

If an excavator excavates
A motivator motivates
An activator activates
A rotivator rotivates
5 A cultivator cultivates
And an operator operates
What does an alligator do?

Michael Rosen

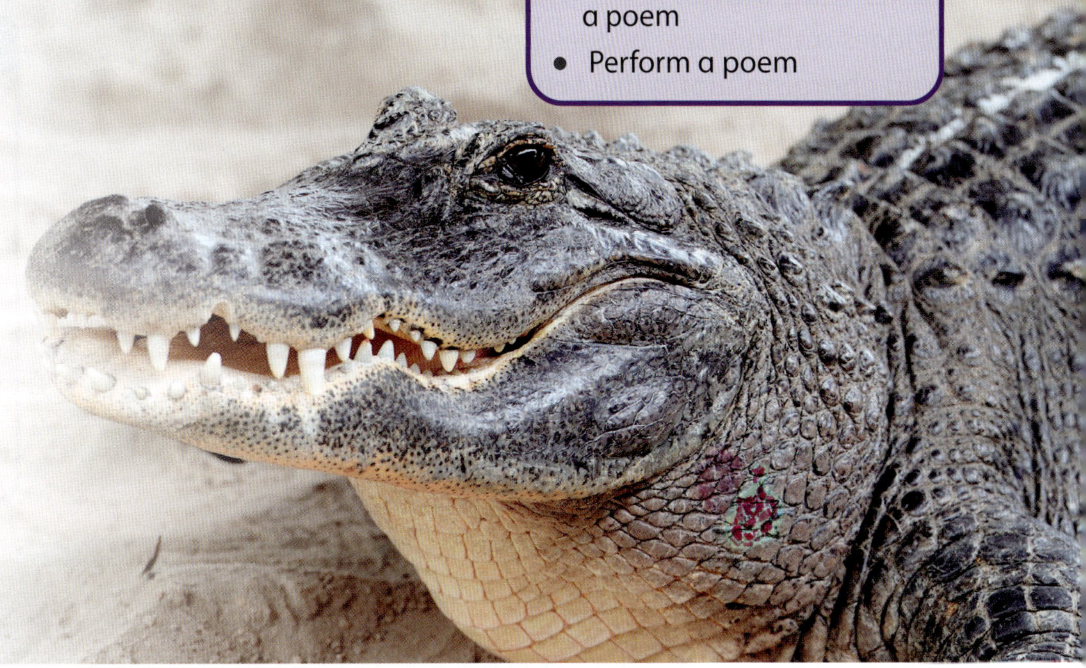

**A** Read the poem 'Alligator Problem' to yourself, quietly. As a class, clap the rhythm as you read the poem aloud, together. What happens to the rhythm when you reach the last two lines?

**B** Some poems are better for performance than others. Which of the features below do you think help to make a good performance poem? Explain your answers.

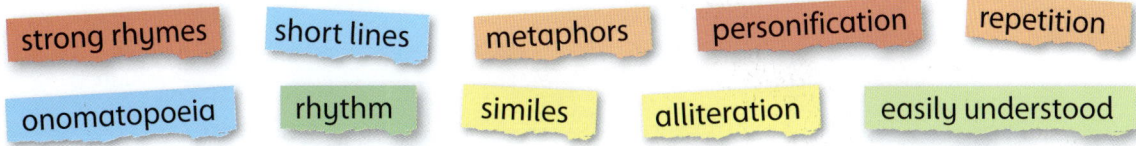

strong rhymes    short lines    metaphors    personification    repetition

onomatopoeia    rhythm    similes    alliteration    easily understood

**C** 1 Which of the following skills do you need to show when reading a performance poem?

- Speak clearly and with expression
- Vary the volume and speed of your voice
- Use expressive body language and hand gestures
- Make eye contact with the audience

2 Read 'Alligator Problem' again as a class, using suitable skills from the list above.

## From a Railway Carriage

Faster than fairies, faster than witches,
Bridges and houses, hedges and ditches;
And charging along like **troops** in a battle
All through the meadows the horses and cattle:
5 All of the sights of the hill and the **plain**
Fly as thick as driving rain;
And ever again, in the wink of an eye,
Painted stations whistle by.

Here is a child who clambers and scrambles,
10 All by himself and gathering **brambles**;
Here is a **tramp** who stands and gazes;
And here is the green for **stringing the daisies**!
Here is a cart runaway in the road
Lumping along with man and load;
15 And here is a mill, and there is a river:
Each a **glimpse** and gone forever!

Robert Louis Stevenson

### Glossary

**troops** group of soldiers
**plain** field
**brambles** prickly bushes
**tramp** person without a home or job
**stringing the daisies** making a chain out of the small white flowers
**glimpse** very quick view

# Comprehension

**A** The poem follows the journey of a steam train as it travels through the countryside. Write answers to these questions.

1  List the things that can be seen from the railway carriage. Look for:

   **a** objects

   **b** people

   **c** animals.

2  The poem has a definite rhythm. What does it make you think of?

- Find details in the poem to answer questions
- Discuss the poem's language, imagery and rhythm
- Perform the poem using speech and non-verbal actions

**B** With a partner, talk about these questions then write down the answers.

1  Why is the train described as 'charging along like troops in a battle'? (line 3)

2  Why did the stations 'whistle by'? (line 8)

3  Line 3 is a simile. Find another simile in the first verse.

4  Find an idiom in the first verse (line 7). What do you think it means?

5  From whose point of view is the poem written?

**C** Perform this poem as a class. You will need to decide:

- who will be passengers
- who will do the sound effects
- who will clap the rhythm
- who will read which part of the poem.

## Poem

The poet Afua Cooper lives in Canada, but she comes from Jamaica.

### Kensington Market

Colours
Colours
Colours everywhere
colours of food
5   and
colours of people
music sounding
music **pounding**
Kensington Market on a Saturday morning.

10 Every Saturday morning
Mom takes her shopping basket
and we go to Kensington Market
Bananas
yams
15 pumpkin
mangos
okras
and
'**whappen**'!
20 Caribbean **scent**.

Afua Cooper

> **Glossary**
>
> **pounding** making a very loud, repeated noise
> **whappen** 'What's happening?' or 'How's it going?'
> **scent** a special smell

148

- Find details in the poem to answer questions
- Discuss the poem's language, the images created, and the rhythm

# Comprehension

**A** Work with a partner to write answers to these questions.

1 What does the poet see in the market?

2 What is the word the poet uses most and why?

3 Find the pairs of words that rhyme.

**B** Write answers to these questions.

1 What effect do the lines with only one word have on the way the poem is read?

2 Why do you think the poet likes this market so much?

3 Why does she use some of the words more than once?

4 Which senses does the poet include?

**C** 1 Imagine you are walking through Kensington Market. Describe it to a partner.

2 Practise reading the poem aloud in small groups. Think carefully about which words you are going to emphasise.

149

# Silent letters

Unstressed letters are not easy to hear and are often silent.

Words like 'language' and 'interested' have **silent vowels** – vowels which are not pronounced. We spell the word like this: **int/er/est/ed**.

But we say the word like this: **in/trest/ed**.

The first **e** becomes silent – int**e**rested

**Learning tip**

Make a list of words with silent letters that you find difficult to spell. Use the strategy in activity C for learning the spellings and see if it works!

**A** Insert the silent **e** or **u** in the words below.

1 bisc __ it
2 temp __ rature
3 g __ ess
4 desp __ rate

5 lit __ rature
6 b __ ilding
7 g __ itar
8 cam __ ra

**B** Find the silent, or almost silent, letters in the words below.

1 hour
2 talk
3 sign
4 often
5 write

6 wrong
7 crumb
8 answer
9 cupboard
10 handsome

**C** With a partner, say each of the words in activities A and B out loud, sounding out all the letters, including the silent ones. Then test each other on how to spell the words **without** sounding out the silent letters.

As a class, talk about all the different strategies you can use to help spell tricky words. Why is it important to be able to spell well? Explain your ideas carefully.

# Countable and uncountable nouns

A **countable noun** can be made into a plural.

*Examples:* tree – trees, country – countries, person – people

If you can give a noun a number, then it is countable.

*Example:* How **many** trees are there? There are **three** trees.

An **uncountable noun** is always singular. It cannot be plural.

*Examples:* water, money, sand.

You can only refer to its amount using general quantifiers such as **some, lots of, a little**.

*Example:* How **much** water is there? There is **a lot**.

**A** With a partner, read the pairs of words below. Decide which noun is countable and which is uncountable. Write them in two lists.

*Example:*      Countable      Uncountable

                car              traffic

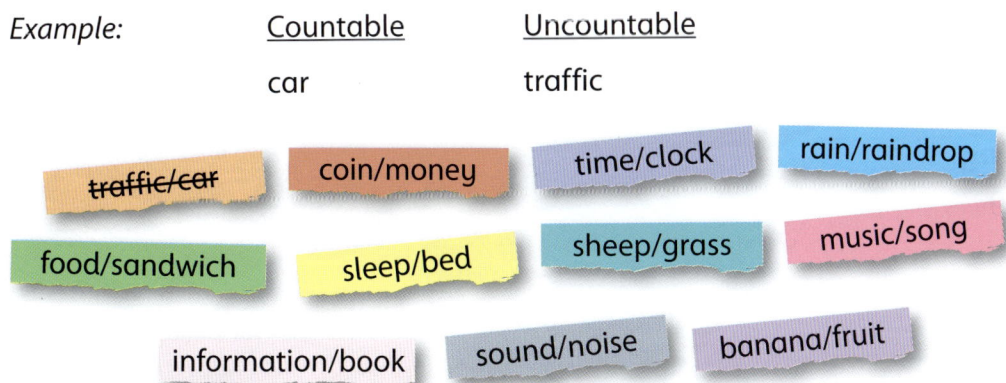

traffic/car    coin/money    time/clock    rain/raindrop

food/sandwich    sleep/bed    sheep/grass    music/song

information/book    sound/noise    banana/fruit

**B** Copy these sentences and write the correct quantifier in each gap.

**1** There are _____ people doing their shopping in the market. (*many/much*)

**2** The passengers saw _____ grass from the train. (*many/lots of*)

**3** Look how _____ steam is coming from the railway engine! (*many/much*)

**4** "Can you see _____ food on the stall?" (*much/four*)

**C** Write four sentences using two countable nouns and two uncountable nouns. Include the correct quantifiers from the list below. Use each quantifier once.

> many     much     two     a little

## Blue Planet's Blue

Boo hoo boo hoo,
Blue planet's **blue**.

Buckets of tears,
**Tsunami** is here.

5 Weep **rant** and wail,
Rhinos for sale.

Cry baby cry,
Forests will die.

Howl, yelp and screech,
10 Oil on the beach.

Watery eyes,
Sea levels rise.

Sob, sigh and whine,
Wildlife on the line.

15 Sighs and **lamenting**,
Climate is changing.

Sing a blue song,
**Habitats** gone.

Boo hoo hoo hoo,
20 Blue planet's real blue.

**Hullabaloo**,
It's all up to you!

Martin Kiszko

**Glossary**

**blue** feels sad

**tsunami** huge sea wave caused by an earthquake

**rant** speak or shout for a long time in an angry way

**lamenting** expressing grief

**habitats** places where animals and plants naturally live

**hullabaloo** a fuss

## Comprehension

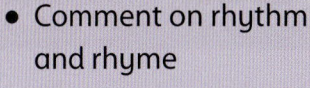

- Comment on rhythm and rhyme
- Find examples of personification and onomatopoeia
- Perform a poem
- Write a poem using a model

**A** Write answers to these questions.

1 What is the rhyming pattern in this poem?

2 What is the main message of the poem?

3 Read the last line. What does it mean?

4 What problems does the poet mention?

5 Find at least six words which sound like the words they describe.

6 The planet is personified in the poem. List all the human actions that the planet displays in the poem.

**B** Read the poem as a class, with individuals or pairs reading one line each.
Pretend to be the planet, performing all the actions found in activity A 6.

**C** 1 In pairs, choose an animal or plant or part of the planet (such as ocean or rainforest) that you want to protect for the future.

2 Write two rhyming lines about the topic you have chosen. Use expressive 'sound' words in your first line, as in the poem on page 152.

3 As a class, write down all the pairs of rhymes on the board until you have your own class Blue Planet poem.

4 Read your lines aloud in pairs around the class, as you did in activity B.

*Example:*   Shout, yell and cry,

Or the tigers will die.

- Write your own rap poem

## I Wanna Be A Star

I **wanna** be a star.
I wanna go far.
I wanna drive around
in a big red car.
I said **yeah** yeah yeah
I wanna be a star.

I wanna **be a hit**.
I wanna be it.
I wanna see my name
all brightly lit.
I said yeah yeah yeah
I wanna be a hit.

I wanna be the scene.
I wanna be on screen.
I wanna make the cover
of a magazine.
I said yeah yeah yeah.
I wanna be the scene.

I wanna be a star.
I wanna go far.
But I've only got a job
in a burger bar –
so far…

Tony Mitton

**Glossary**

**wanna** informal for 'I want to'

**yeah** informal word for 'yes'

**be a hit** be popular and famous

154

## Write your own rap

1 Practise reading the poem together, keeping the rhythm by clapping the beat to begin with. Change the volume and expression in your voice throughout the poem.

## Guided writing

2 You are going to write about something you would you like to be. A doctor? An aeroplane pilot? An athlete?

Write your rap with a partner or in a small group. Decide whether to include some non-standard English, such as the words and phrases 'I wanna be' and 'yeah'.

Remember to include:

- rhyme
- rhythm

Look back at activity B on page 145 for other ideas about what to include in your poem to make it fun and easy to perform.

3 Clap your rap as you write. Read your first draft aloud and, if it doesn't sound right, change it.

## Perform your rap

4 Look back at activity C on page 145 for ideas about how to perform a poem. Everyone should have a part in the performance. When you have all learned your parts and rehearsed enough, perform your rap in front of the class. Remember to make eye contact with the audience and think about how you could get the audience involved in the performance. Find out if it's possible for it to be videoed.

- Perform the rap using different voices and actions
- Discuss the language style in rap lyrics
- Write verses for a rap poem in the same style

# Revise and check (3)

## Vocabulary

**1** Make a list of the words in the phrases below which have a silent letter when they are spoken. Circle the silent letter of each word. Write a sentence for each phrase.

**a** chilli chocolate

**b** correct answers

**c** rustling papers

**d** low temperatures

**e** vegetable curry

**f** half a tomato

**2** Match the synonyms below. The first one has been done for you. Add another synonym to each pair.

say ——————— chilly

eat ————————→ declare

walk　　　　　　scorching

hot　　　　　　　gobble

cold　　　　　　　creep

**3** Match the phrases and words to complete the idioms. Write a sentence including each idiom, showing its meaning.

rags to　　　　　　neck

piece of　　　　　　riches

neck and　　　　　　cake

## Punctuation

**1** Write out the sentences below and add commas in the right places.

**a** A boy sat on the shore of a deep blue lake.

**b** "Oh what are we going to do?"

**c** Next morning Tchang's mother knew just what to do.

**d** Since she was born she hasn't spoken a word.

# Grammar

**1** Rewrite each sentence below, adding a prepositional phrase from the list.

> behind the station    in the mountains    by train

  **a**  The family decided to take a holiday _____.

  **b**  They travelled together _____.

  **c**  They found the hotel _____.

**2** Replace the underlined words with pronouns.

  **a**  <u>Felix</u> met his friends and went to the park.

  **b**  <u>The family</u> stayed in the cottage that belonged to Grandmother Betty.

  **c**  "Don't touch the computer," <u>Aunt Ase</u> said. "It's Grandma's."

**3** Rewrite the sentences below, choosing the correct words.

  **a**  Where/wear are there/their boots?

  **b**  We're not going there/they're today.

  **c**  We're/where coming to/too!

# Spelling

**1** Rewrite the sentences below, using the correct form of the verbs.

Kirsty was (carry) a heavy parcel. Fin ran up and (grab) it from her.
Kirsty (gasp). "I'm (try) to help," he told her. Then Fin (drop) the parcel!

**2** Choose the correct prefix and write the opposites of these words.

> un-   dis-   in-   il-   ir-   im-

  **a**  legible          **d**  belief          **e**  possible

  **b**  visible          **c**  comfortable          **f**  regular

**3**  Write a sentence for each of the above words.

157

### The Tale of Custard the Dragon

Belinda lived in a little white house,
With a little black kitten and a little gray mouse,
And a little yellow dog and a little red wagon,
And a realio, trulio, little pet dragon.

5 Now the name of the little black kitten was Ink,
And the little gray mouse, her name was Blink,
And the little yellow dog was sharp as Mustard,
But the dragon was a coward, and she called him Custard.

Custard the dragon had big sharp teeth,
10 And spikes on top of him and scales underneath,
Mouth like a fireplace, chimney for a nose,
And realio, trulio daggers on his toes.

Belinda was as brave as a barrel-full of bears,
And Ink and Blink chased lions down the stairs,
15 Mustard was as brave as a tiger in a rage,
But Custard cried for a nice safe cage.

Belinda tickled him, she tickled him unmerciful,
Ink, Blink and Mustard, they rudely called him Percival,
They all sat laughing in the little red wagon
20 At the realio, trulio, cowardly dragon.

Belinda giggled till she shook the house,
And Blink said Weeek!, which is giggling for a mouse,
Ink and Mustard rudely asked his age,
When Custard cried for a nice safe cage.

25 Suddenly, suddenly they heard a nasty sound,
And Mustard growled, and they all looked around.
Meowch! cried Ink, and Ooh! cried Belinda,
For there was a pirate, climbing in the winda.

Pistol in his left hand, pistol in his right,
30 And he held in his teeth a **cutlass** bright;
His beard was black, one leg was wood.
It was clear that the pirate meant no good.

Belinda paled, and she cried Help! Help!
But Mustard fled with a terrified yelp,
35 Ink trickled down to the bottom of the household,
And little mouse Blink **strategically mouseholed**.

But up jumped Custard, snorting like an engine,
Clashed his tail like irons in a dungeon,
With a clatter and a clank and a jangling squirm
40 He went at the pirate like a robin at a worm.

The pirate gaped at Belinda's dragon,
And gulped some **grog** from his pocket **flagon**,
He fired two bullets, but they didn't hit,
And Custard gobbled him, every bit.

### Glossary

**cutlass** short sword with a wide, curved blade

**strategically mouseholed** decided it was safer to go back to his home

**grog** favourite drink of pirates

**flagon** container for drinks

45 Belinda embraced him, Mustard licked him;
No one mourned for his pirate victim.
Ink and Blink in **glee** did **gyrate**,
Around the dragon that ate the pirate.

Belinda still lives in her little white house,
50 With her little black kitten and her little gray mouse,
And her little yellow dog and her little red wagon,
And her realio, trulio, little pet dragon.

Belinda is as brave as a barrel-full of bears,
And Ink and Blink chase lions down the stairs,
55 Mustard is as brave as a tiger in a rage,
But Custard keeps crying for a nice safe cage.

Ogden Nash